MW00574933

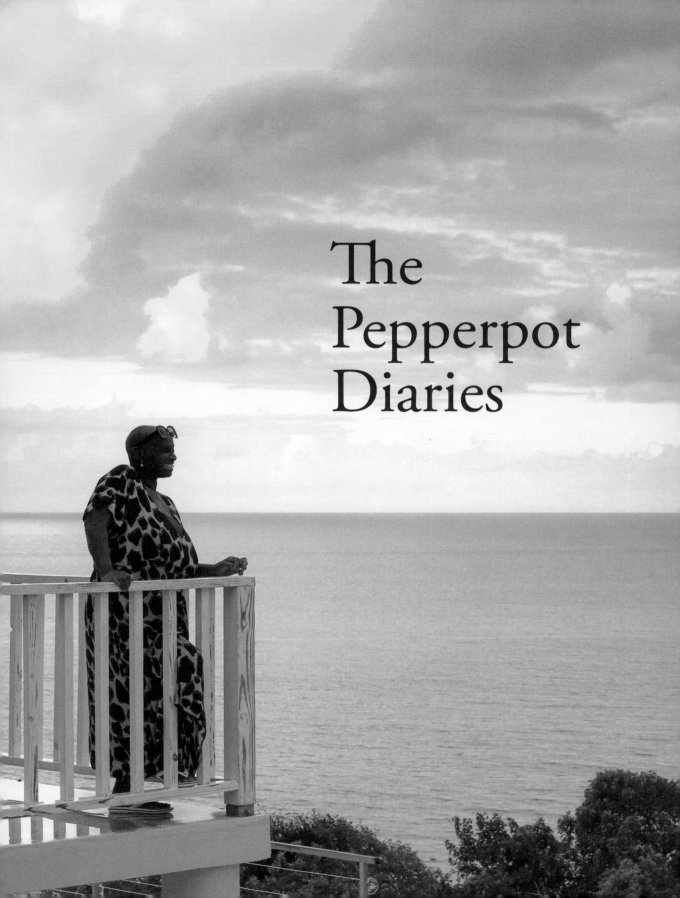

The
Pepperpot
Diaries

The Pepperpot Diaries

Stories from my Caribbean table

ANDI OLIVER

Contents

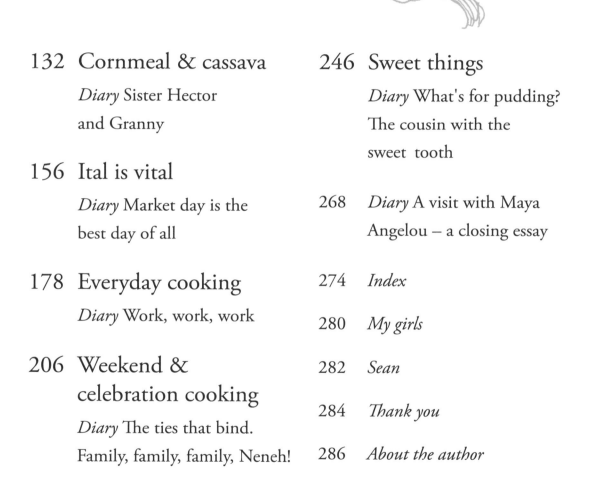

Stories from my Caribbean table

The Pepperpot Diaries is a book that has been swirling around me for years. I now find myself here in Antigua, with finally some time and space to start getting these thoughts down onto paper. Exploring the flavours that I grew up with, this book is indeed a little walk across the Caribbean islands themselves, but it's also a walk through me. I am a mix of that which my mother, father, aunties, and uncles all brought with them when they came to England.

I am also one of those who was made here, made in the new but somehow still steeped in the old. It's somewhere way down inside me though; not really knowing that deep truth about myself, but always looking over my shoulder feeling like I'd left the gas on or left something behind. There is a veracity to this for most all of the daughters and sons of migrant families. It becomes diluted over the years and generations, but I feel that, somehow, we are always looking back trying to work out how to become grounded. This is why our food and the kitchen is so important to us. It directly connects us to the other place, where we can feel the sun on our skin and hear the pots banging, feel the concentration down the ages as ingenuity and needs must, conspired to create a culinary lexicon that is precious and life-saving.

The Caribbean is not just one place, it is many places, many stories, many people. And we each have our own way of cooking, our own way of telling those stories, our own way of bringing flavour to the plate.

Caribbean food is a direct result of the feet that have trodden through the islands. The DNA from those who have come and gone and stayed is not just in our blood, it is in our food. There is, of course, a dark shadow in the story, but in our food, there is light and joy and survival and colour. Influences from India, Spain, the Americas, Africa, China, Portugal, Britain, France, and not forgetting the indigenous inhabitants – the Taino, the Arawaks, the Caribs.

It is truly a global cuisine, constantly evolving and bursting with flavour. I am a mix of all these things, and, I am a Black British woman, which brings in yet another voice, another layer to the story, another flavour to the pot.

This book is my way of telling just some of those stories, my way of singing my song. A bit of the past, the present, and the future. As always, with love from me to you,

For the immersive Pepperpot Diaries experience listen along to my curated playlist here

7

A note to the cook

The recipes in this book are very dear to me. They have direction, clear instructions, photos, and measurements, and I've spent a long time getting them just right, so they hit that glorious spot that we all love so much – that moment in the kitchen when the textures, spices, temperatures, and flavours are working their magic in harmony, and all is right with the world.

I feel that I want these recipes to be just the start for you. I'd love you to think of them as a jumping off point. Some recipes refer to old-school ways of doing things, which some of you may recognize, but others come completely from the reaches of my own imagination. I believe that cooking is a personal adventure, but to feel free enough to step into any adventure you need to first find your confidence.

I've been cooking since I was a kid, and I've discovered that once you've made enough things that you thought were mistakes – but which actually turned out to be wonderful – that anything is possible in the kitchen. For me, the way forward is not to look to impress, but just to find what is delicious. That way, you will actually impress guests when you want to, but also, and for me this is a hugely important part, you will comfort and nourish yourself, as well as those you're cooking for.

Think of the things you are yearning for, step towards the flavours you love and 9 times out of 10, you'll get food onto your plate that was well worth the effort. Every single time that happens, you gain a little more confidence. What about that other one time I hear you ask? When a culinary accident comes knocking at the door which doesn't turn out to be delicious, I say, don't worry, it's only dinner. Don't let it upset you, learn from your mistake and get right back on your cooking horse!

So, I want you to think of the recipes in this book as templates, not direct orders from on high. Think of them as your friend in the kitchen, having a chat with you about what's going to end up on the table for breakfast, lunch, or dinner.

Some recipes have been created with those fly-by days in mind, when you barely have time to think about cooking, but you still need to feed yourself or you and those you love. There are also recipes for those long, leisurely drawn-out cooking days, when you have a glass of something perfect in your hand, the tunes are rolling, and you have all day to make something spectacular (the important part here is that it shouldn't be stressful!).

It's all in the planning, dear readers. Stick with me and whatever your mood, we'll get there together.

MAM

"SIMPL

B

FUNGI

SALTFISH

DUKANA

SOUP

BEV*

THE
EST!

LOCAL ♥ JUICES

ER/P♥T

ASONED RICE

RATED
#1

Let's talk pepperpots

I have chosen to start with two versions of a classic Caribbean recipe that are very close to my heart; so close they became the title of this book. The name of the dish – pepperpot – is heavy with significance for me. Firstly, it evokes my grandmother, whose recipe I still use. It also signifies family lineage, history, ancestry, and connection.

Pepperpots are perfect examples of what can be made with ingredients that were once deemed not good enough for the high table. This kind of cooking is truly extraordinary to me; it shows the African hand, it shows the spirit of the powerful souls of enslaved ones still reaching for beauty and striving to bring love to each other... cooking to bring family together when it's been torn apart. To me, it says no matter what you leave us with, no matter what you do to us, we will still create, we will still love and nourish each other. I find this so moving, it is so much more than just meat and vegetables in a pot.

In my family and in Caribbean culture in general, meals made in one big, deep pot are commonplace. Large family gatherings usually have at least one big-pot dish on the table that's full of powerful flavours and probably took a day or two to cook. The quantities may seem a bit daunting, but I want you to think of them as an adventure. Once you've got your head around the organization of ingredients, it's actually an easy way to feed a celebratory throng. Once it's all in, it's just about time rather than lots of faffing, which is why I would advocate making the pot the day before you need it. This gives the flavours a chance to sit and develop and become even more delectable.

With both these pepperpot recipes (and a couple of the other dishes in this book), I would just never make a tiny amount. The whole point of them is great abundance, and nourishing a big table full of people. If there are fewer people at your table and it seems ridiculous, then perhaps split leftovers up and freeze them in batches. I really do urge you to go big, but if it's just an unfathomable idea for you, then simply split all the ingredient quantities in half and bring it down in size that way.

For the rest of you? Let's GO!

Mamma's pepperpot

1.5kg (3lb 3oz) salt beef (corned beef)

4 salted pig's tails

1 oxtail, cut into 2.5cm (1in) pieces

1 smoked ham hock

1 x 330ml (11fl oz) bottle of stout

For smoking

4 cinnamon sticks, broken up

2 tsp black peppercorns

2 tsp white peppercorns

2 tsp cumin seeds

2 tsp whole allspice

4 tbsp breakfast tea leaves

For the stew

500g (3 cups) dried black-eyed beans
(black-eyed peas)

3 onions, thinly sliced

3 medium tomatoes, roughly chopped

3 celery sticks, thinly sliced

handful of celery leaves, roughly chopped

1 Scotch bonnet, seeds removed if you
prefer less heat

6 sprigs of thyme

750g (1lb 10oz) okra, trimmed and quartered

3 aubergines (eggplants), cut into 2.5cm
(1in) pieces

4 bunches of spinach, stems removed and
roughly shredded

2 bunches of chard, roughly shredded

salt and freshly ground black pepper

To garnish

thinly sliced fried okra

stovetop smoker (see Note to reader)

Serves 12 or more
Prep time 1 hour, plus overnight soaking
Cook time 4½ hours

In its Antiguan permutation, pepperpot is made with salt pork, salt beef, pig tails, and in my grandma's version even smoked oxtail (sooo good). We also tend to use a LOT of greens in ours, running spinach (also known as callaloo), chard, kale, eddoe tops, okra, and really anything else green you can get your hands on.

The night before cooking, soak the salt beef and salted pig's tails in plenty of water. Soak the black-eyed beans in a separate bowl. Keep both in the fridge overnight.

The next day, add all the smoking ingredients to the bottom of a stovetop smoker (or see Note to reader, opposite). Add the oxtail to the rack in the smoker and close the lid. Put the smoker over a medium heat for 7 minutes, then switch off the heat and leave the lid on for 15 minutes, until all the smoke has disappeared.

Drain the soaked salt beef and pig's tails, discarding the water. Skin the pig's tails and ham hock and cut these and the salt beef into 2.5cm (1in) pieces. Add all the meat (including the smoked oxtail) to a large pot. Pour over the stout and enough water to cover all the ingredients. Bring to the boil, then turn the heat down to medium–low and simmer for 3 hours, or until the meat is tender. Top up the pot with enough water to keep the meat covered as it cooks, and skim away any froth that floats to the surface.

Drain the soaked beans. When the meat is tender, remove it from the pot with tongs or a slotted spoon and set it aside. To the same cooking liquid in the pot, add the drained beans, onions, tomatoes, celery, celery leaves, Scotch bonnet, and thyme and give the pot a good stir. Finally, add the okra and top up the pot with enough water to cover, if needed. Do not stir at this point, otherwise the okra will sink to the bottom and burn.

Leave to bubble away and cook for about 1½ hours, or until the beans are tender.

Meanwhile, add the aubergine, 3 bunches of the spinach, and the chard to a pan of boiling water. Cook for about 5–6 minutes until soft, then drain well, reserving the cooking liquid for later if needed. Let the vegetables cool slightly, then roughly chop them together.

When the beans are cooked, add the cooked chopped vegetables and the meat back into the pot. Give everything a good stir, let it heat through and season with salt and pepper. Finally, add the remaining bunch of chopped spinach to the pot and let it wilt.

Serve scattered with thinly sliced fried okra.

Note to reader

*If you don't have a smoker at home you can make one.
First, layer your spices or smoking materials in the bottom of a roasting tin. Next, take a metal oven rack and wrap it in tin foil. Poke a few holes in the foil with a skewer or pin and lay the rack in the roasting tray over the smoking materials. Place the food you are smoking (in this case the oxtails) on top of the foil covered rack, then cover the whole tray and the food with foil again, leaving no gaps. Place the whole thing on the hob (stove) over a low heat for around 7–8 minutes – longer if you like a very deep smoke flavour or less time if you're smoking something delicate like seafood or vegetables.*

Guyanese pepperpot

Serves 15–20
Prep time 20–30 minutes, plus marinating time
Cook time about 5 hours

The same effort and love is, of course, required for the Guyanese pepperpot. Their version is darker and rich with cassareep. Once again, royal perfection.

2kg (4½lb) diced bone-in braising steak, mutton, pork, oxtail, or any combination of these you like

800g (1¾lb) pork knuckle chopped small (optional, a butcher can chop this for you)

4 tbsp Green Seasoning (see page 110)

1 tbsp ground allspice

2 tsp ground coriander

2 tsp ground turmeric

2 tsp ground cumin

1 tsp ground ginger

6 tbsp rapeseed (canola) oil

250g (9oz) white onions, chopped or blitzed in a food processor

4 garlic cloves, grated

1–2 wiri wiri chilli(es), Scotch bonnet, or habanero, to taste

3 sprigs of thyme

grated zest from 1 orange

4 cinnamon sticks

1 tbsp whole black cardamom pods

1 tsp whole cloves

120g (½ cup) light or dark brown soft sugar

2 tsp salt

2 tsp black pepper

1 litre (4⅓ cups) beef or chicken stock

250ml (1 cup plus 1 tbsp) cassareep or blackstrap molasses

To begin, wash the meat in a solution made with water and a splash of lemon juice or white vinegar – this step is entirely optional, but it is considered key in Caribbean culture. Pat the meat dry with kitchen paper (paper towels).

Add the diced meat to a large bowl with the green seasoning, allspice, coriander, turmeric, cumin, and ginger. Mix well, cover the bowl with cling film (plastic wrap) and leave to marinate in the fridge for at least 2 hours, or ideally overnight.

Set a large saucepan or casserole dish over a medium–high heat and add the oil. Working in batches, brown off the marinated meat and pork knuckle (if using). Keep a roasting tray next to the hob (stove) and as each batch is browned, transfer the meat to the tray and reserve to one side.

When all the meat is browned and the pan is empty, add the onion, garlic, and chilli(es) and sauté for a few minutes until slightly softened. Add all the meat back into the pan, along with the thyme, orange zest, cinnamon, cardamom, cloves, sugar, and salt and pepper.

Give the pan a good stir, then pour in the stock and 1 litre (4⅓ cups) of water. Turn the heat up and bring to a gentle boil. Use a spoon to skim away any froth that rises to the top.

Add the cassareep or molasses and once again reduce the heat to low, cover, and simmer very gently for around 4 hours or until the meat is meltingly tender. Remove the lid and simmer for 1 further hour or so, until the sauce has reduced to a rich, thick, glossy consistency and the meat is so soft that it's falling off the bone. Serve hot.

Note to reader

The heritage recipes within this book all come from an oral tradition, and were created at a time when most people were not necessarily able to read or write. A lot was dependent on family dialect and the particular island vernacular, so you'll often find different spellings or names for the same dish from different people.

Bread & dumplings

Tonight, I had quite possibly the BEST fried dumplings I've ever had. The deep-fried Jamaican kind anyway! My gorgeous cousin, Zufana, (also known as Queenie for obvious regal-like bearing reasons) presented us with a mountain of golden, crisp, LIGHT, and fluffy globes of perfection. It really got me thinking about the many permutations of dumplings that weave their way through the Caribbean… festivals, fried dumplings, Johnny cakes, ducana, coconut dumplings, bakes, droppers, duff. This makes my mind run on all the many breads too… rotis, puris, buss up shot, coco bread. They're ALL used to mop up gravy, sauces, and stews and all the delicious bits in the corners of dishes. So here we go, off down the dumpling and bread highway.

Friday 8th January

Gerry & Zufana

Thus begins an intermittent journal of my three-month trip to Antigua. Today I'm in the outdoor kitchen at the big house we're staying in at Turtle Bay. It is Rasta Christmas, and my dear cousin Gerry and his ridiculously fabulous wife, Zufana (queen of the fried dumplings and many other things) are coming over.

Yesterday when we were driving up the main road from St. John's, I screeched to a halt because out of the corner of my eye I spied a table groaning under the weight of a fresh ackee harvest! Just piles of them. "How much?" I asked. "$5 a heap," she said. It took a minute to ascertain that a "heap" meant about five pods of them... so I just bought them all in the end. I figured that once Zufana shows me how to prep them (it's really quite tricky because there is a pink papery bit that is hard to get out and is properly toxic, as in not just make you sick but can kill you!), we'll cook half and whack the rest in the freezer for later.

I've discovered that ackee DOES grow in Antigua. I was under the impression that it only grew in Jamaica, because really and truly Jamaicans are the people who really love to eat them. People here in Antigua don't really cook them, in fact the lady I bought them off said she doesn't really eat ackee. She doesn't even *really* like them, but she may as well pick the fruit and sell it she can... most times people just leave them for the birds to eat!

Oh gosh, though, I just LOOOOOVE me some ackee!

ON THE MENU TODAY

ACKEE, CALLALOO, & SALTFISH

FRIED DUMPLINGS

Ackee, callaloo, & saltfish

Serves 6
Prep time 20 minutes
Cook time 30 minutes

I think the thing I love most about ackee is its amazing, surprising creaminess. This dish, a version of the classic Jamaican ackee and saltfish with gorgeous spinach or callaloo running through it, is comforting and nutritious in equal measures.

1 x medium pack (about 454g/1lb) skinless and boneless saltfish, such as ling, cod, or pollock

3½ tbsp rapeseed (canola) oil

1 onion, thinly sliced

4 garlic cloves, finely grated

3 chillies of your choice, finely chopped

50g (1¾oz) red or green sweet peppers, deseeded and thinly sliced

200g (7oz) cherry tomatoes, halved, or use roughly chopped medium tomatoes

300g (10oz) callaloo or spinach

500g (1lb 2oz) fresh or canned ackee, drained if canned (see page 22 for an important fresh preparation tip)

First, rinse the saltfish thoroughly, then put it into a pot and cover with fresh cold water. Bring to the boil, then drain the water. Repeat this boiling process twice more using fresh water each time to get rid of the excess salt. Set the fish aside in a bowl to cool.

Once cooled, flake the fish gently with a fork until no large chunks remain and set aside.

Add the oil to a heavy-based, high sided frying pan set over a medium–low heat. Add the onion, garlic, and chilli and fry gently until softened. Add the sweet peppers to the pan and let them cook down for a further 10 minutes, stirring occasionally. Add the tomatoes and cook down for a further 5–6 minutes.

Add the prepared saltfish and VERY gently turn it through the onions and whatnot in the pan – be very gentle here because you don't want to mush the fish up. Let the fish cook for a couple more minutes, then lay the callaloo or spinach on top. Let the callaloo or spinach gently wilt into the rest of the ingredients, then stir through.

Lastly, lay the ackee very gently on top. Cover the pan with a lid and leave it to warm through for 10 minutes before gently folding through. Serve with Fried Dumplings (see page 31).

Fried dumplings

Serves 6
Prep time 10 minutes, plus 1–2 hours resting time
Cook time 8–10 minutes

I love dumplings of all persuasions. There are so many dumpling iterations across the Caribbean, but this Jamaican variety is possibly the most well-known.

150g (1 cup plus 2 tbsp) self-raising flour, plus extra for dusting

1 tsp baking powder

good, fat pinch of salt

good, fat pinch of white granulated sugar

2 tsp unsalted butter, at room temperature

500ml (generous 2 cups) neutral oil, such as rapeseed (canola) or sunflower oil, for deep-frying

Combine the flour, baking powder, salt, and sugar in a medium bowl. Add the room temperature butter and use your hands to rub it into the dry ingredients.

Little by little, pour about 100–110ml (generous ⅓ cup) water into the bowl, mixing with your hand with each addition until a dough forms. It is important not to overwork the dough here – it will be soft, but this is what will make the dumplings soft on the inside and crispy on the outside. Cover the dough in the bowl with cling film (plastic wrap) and leave to rest at room temperature for about 1–2 hours (2 hours if you have time).

Dust a work surface with a small amount of flour and gently knead the dough through. Divide the dough into six pieces. Using floured palms, roll each piece of dough into a ball and set aside.

Heat the oil in a deep-fat fryer or heavy-based saucepan to 180°C (350°F). To test whether the oil is hot enough, drop in a cube of white bread. If it bubbles straight away and goes golden, then the oil is ready for frying.

Gently slip half the batch of dough balls into the hot oil and fry for about 8–10 minutes, gently rotating the balls as they fry to ensure an even, golden finish. Remove from the oil with a slotted spoon and place on a plate lined with kitchen paper (paper towels) to drain any excess oil and cool slightly. Repeat the frying process with the remaining dough.

Enjoy the dumplings while they are warm.

Ducana

Makes 12
Prep time 25 minutes
Cook time 45–60 minutes

Oh dear Lord – I am a staunchly irreligious individual, but these boiled coconut dumplings are the kind of food that makes me reach for prayer!! They're subtly flavoured parcels of coconutty delight, which act as a gentle and welcome accompaniment to any kind of main dish you're eating. Excellent with a traditional Antiguan breakfast of saltfish and chop-up (see page 82), or alongside a fiery hot curry. Alternatively, try them with some of the slow-roast pork dishes in this book, like the Green Seasoning & Rum Porchetta (see page 112) or the Vinidaloush (see page 270)... have at it! They are truly divine.

200g (2⅔ cups) desiccated (dried shredded) coconut

300ml (1¼ cups) coconut milk

2 tsp white sugar

pinch of nutmeg

2 tsp salt

1 tsp vanilla extract

275g (9¾oz) white sweet potatoes

190g (scant 1½ cups) plain (all-purpose) flour

12 green banana leaves, warmed over an open flame to make them more pliable, for cooking (optional)

Add the desiccated coconut, coconut milk, sugar, nutmeg, salt, and vanilla to a bowl. Stir together and leave to soak for 15–20 minutes at room temperature.

Meanwhile, peel and grate the sweet potatoes.

Add the grated sweet potatoes and flour to the soaked coconut. Stir to combine all of the ingredients well. The mixture should be a bit sticky – don't add any more flour or this will make the dumplings hard.

Bring a large saucepan of water to the boil.

Depending on how big you want your ducana, measure a level or heaped tablespoon of mixture into your hand and mould this into an approx. 10 x 15cm (6 x 4in) rectangle. Place the rectangle into a banana leaf (if using) or a piece of tin foil and wrap it up tightly. If using banana leaves, use strips of the centre vein of the leaf or pieces of cooking string/twine to tie the packets up. If using tin foil, this should hold on its own.

Add all the wrapped pieces to the pot of boiling water. There should be enough water to completely cover all the parcels.

Boil for 45–60 minutes until the parcels rise to the top and the dumpling mixture inside is firm and robust. Remove from the water and allow to cool before unwrapping and serving alongside your favourite dish.

Easy peasy roti stylee

Serves 8
Prep time 20 minutes, plus 30 minutes resting time
Cook time 30 minutes

This is one of those recipes that connects us to the meeting of race, creed, and culture across the Caribbean. The heritage version dates back to 12th century India, but varieties such as buss up shot, roti and paratha are all now a familiar part of the Caribbean dinner table, perfect for mopping up gravies, spiced butters, and curries.

My dad used to LOVE cricket – he didn't seem to care that he was terrible at it (at least that's how I remember it!). He was probably there more for the rum and mates, really. The best bit about cricket for me, though, was the picnic. In particular, the rotis from my much-adored Antiguan Aunt Gwen Bryan. Soft, freshly made breads filled with golden curries that dribbled down your chin when you ate them – heaven!

I am very keen on this quick roti recipe variation, which my friend and our Wadadli Kitchen Head Chef Sacha Henry showed me. Sacha himself adapted the recipe from his Punjabi grandmother, Bhajno. You can bash the finished breads up, so you have what we call "buss up shot" roti, or leave them whole and pile them high.

350g (2⅔ cups) self-raising flour, plus extra for dusting

1 level tsp baking powder

1 big pinch of caster (granulated) sugar

2 big pinches of salt

250g (generous 1 cup) full-fat plain yogurt
    (or use coconut yogurt for dairy-free)

about 10–12 tbsp softened unsalted butter

Combine the flour, baking powder, sugar, salt, and yogurt in a large mixing bowl. Use your hands to give it a good thorough mix up and bring it all together to make a dough.

Tip the dough out onto a lightly floured work surface and knead it through for 2–3 minutes until smooth. Form the dough into a ball, wrap in cling film (plastic wrap) and leave to rest in the bowl for 30 minutes at room temperature.

Lightly dust a work surface with flour again. Unwrap the dough and separate it into 8 portions of around 80g (2¾oz) each (this bit is not an exact science, so if you end up with a different number of portions it's fine). Roll each portion of dough into a ball. Next, use a rolling pin to roll each ball out into a rough rectangle. Spread or brush each rectangle with 1 generous tablespoon of butter. Fold in each side of the rectangle, then the bottom and the top to roughly form a little square shape. Turn the square of dough over and over in your hands, lightly pressing the edges of the square down against the work surface until the shape becomes rounded into an irregular circle.

Use the rolling pin to roll each circle of dough out again into a rough rectangle shape. Smear each with a teaspoon of butter, then fold each end in again. Finally, begin to gently roll out each dough rectangle into a bigger circle, around the size of an average dinner plate – some of the butter may squoosh out of the sides here, which is kind of unavoidable. Dust with a little more flour as you go to keep the roti from sticking.

Heat a heavy-based frying pan over a high heat until almost smoking hot. Slip in your first roti and slightly lower the heat to medium–high. Cook until golden underneath and a few tiny air pockets appear on top, then flip over onto the other side. Brush with a little more butter, then when golden underneath too, flip over and brush with more butter. After 1–2 final minutes, transfer the roti from the pan to a plate. Repeat until you have used all your dough, stacking the rotis up on the plate and brushing a little more butter between each one as you go. Cover with a kitchen towel to keep warm until ready to serve.

Bakes

Makes 5–10, depending on size
Prep time 15 minutes, plus 10–15 minutes
resting time
Cook time 10–20 minutes

This bake is a kissing cousin of the Johnny cake, which is what I grew up eating. The cooking method for the bake is slightly different to the Johnny cake, and there is the optional addition of coconut milk here (erm, yes please!), which also sets these two apart. Despite their subtle differences, the comforting familiarity of a bake still brings me back to my mum's table.

550g (scant 4¼ cups) plain (all-purpose) flour
   or bread flour, plus extra for dusting

4 tsp baking powder

1 tsp salt

2 tbsp slightly softened butter

375ml (generous 1½ cups) water
   or coconut milk

about 100ml (generous ⅓ cup) neutral oil,
   such as rapeseed (canola) or sunflower oil,
   for frying, plus extra for oiling the dough

Combine the flour, baking powder, and salt in a large mixing bowl. Add the softened butter and mix until evenly distributed. Gradually add the water or coconut milk, bit by bit, mixing with each addition until a soft, slightly sticky dough starts to form.

Tip the dough out onto a floured work surface and knead for a few minutes until somewhat smooth. Place the dough back in the bowl, rub with a small amount of oil and cover with a damp kitchen towel. Let the dough rest for 10–15 minutes.

Heat the oil in a deep, heavy-based pan to 180–200°C (350–400°F). To test whether the oil is hot enough, drop in a piece of dough. If it bubbles straight away and goes golden, then the oil is ready for frying.

Place the rested dough on a lightly floured work surface and knead it through for 1 minute. Divide the dough into 5–10 equal portions (depending on what size you'd like), rolling each portion into a small ball. Slightly flatten each dough ball with the palm of your hand.

Lower the dough balls gently into the hot oil, being careful not to overcrowd the pan. Using a long-handled heatproof spoon, gently baste the floating dough balls with the hot oil, which will encourage them to puff up slightly. Once puffed, flip the dough balls over and cook on the other side until they are lightly golden brown.

Remove the bakes from the oil with a slotted spoon and place on a plate lined with kitchen paper (paper towels) to drain the excess oil. Repeat the cooking process with any remaining dough and serve straight away.

The dough can also be baked (as is traditional in Trinidad), if you prefer. Preheat the oven to 170–175°C fan (190°C/375°F/

Gas 5) and line a baking sheet with baking parchment. Space the dough balls out on the lined baking sheet and bake in the preheated oven for 20–25 minutes until lightly golden brown, or until the base of each bake sounds hollow when tapped.

Note to reader

A street food staple across many of the Caribbean isles, including Guyana, Grenada, Barbados, and Saint Lucia as well as Trinidad and Tobago. When baked in an oven or cooked on a traditional stovetop griddle (tawah), these are known as "bake bake" or "roast bake". When fried they are referred to as "floats", "fried bakes" or simply "fry bake".

Despite their ubiquity and regional variation (for example, the Bajan iteration tends to be a fried wet batter, more akin to a fritter or hush puppy) the core recipe is believed to have similar roots to those of its counterparts such as quick bread or Johnny cakes. It is said to have originally been a much simpler recipe due to the level of deprivation experienced by colonized and enslaved Caribbeans; recipes containing additions such as baking powder, butter, spices, etc. were once considered extreme luxury.

In Grenada and Trinidad and Tobago in particular, bakes are popularly served alongside or filled with saltfish buljol, or fried and breaded shark fillets (often Atlantic blacktip) – one of the more sustainably fished sharks in the world – marinated in Green Seasoning, showcasing a little of the interesting versatility in Caribbean cuisine.

Bolon de verde

Makes 10
Prep time 15 minutes
Cook time 15–30 minutes

This dish came to Ecuador through Cuba and has a direct line to the enslaved African population of that island. The name literally means big ball of green – and that green is green plantain fried dumplings. For me, these are a triumph of salty meat and cheese and the starchy plantain; they make a brilliant platter to bring to a celebration table. In South American Caribbean regions, plantain is eaten green AND ripe, and it's a whole new delicious world. This recipe is a gorgeous introduction to the world of the green plantain!

4 green plantains or bananas

salt, to taste

240g (8½oz) crumbled queso fresco, or an alternative fresh/semi-hard cheese such as feta, cotija, ricotta salata, etc. (use half this amount if using extra cheese in the stuffing)

neutral oil, such as rapeseed (canola) or sunflower oil, for frying

Optional extras

4 tbsp butter or lard, roughly chopped

120g (4½oz) crumbled queso fresco, or an alternative of your choice (see above)

1 onion, diced and sautéed

200g (7oz) pork meat, bacon, or dry chorizo, diced and fried

additional herbs and spices of your choice such as black pepper, cumin, cayenne pepper, fresh chilli, coriander, etc.

Cut off the ends of each green plantain or banana, peel and chop them into roughly equal sized chunks. Cook the plantain or bananas either by boiling them in slightly salted water for about 20 minutes until fork tender, or by frying them in a little oil for about 10 minutes until soft and lightly golden brown.

Once they are cooked, drain, then mash the plantain/bananas in a bowl with salt to taste. Allow to cool slightly before adding the cheese and any optional extra filling items you have chosen (or you can choose to stuff the balls with the extra filling items in the next step). Mix and then knead the mixture to form a dough-like consistency. Shape into roughly 10 equally sized balls – now stuffing the balls further with extra fillings at this point if you wish.

Heat the oil in a deep-fat fryer or heavy-based saucepan to 170–175°C (340–350°F). To test whether the oil is hot enough, drop in a cube of white bread. If it bubbles straight away and goes golden, then the oil is ready for frying. Fry the plantain balls in batches until they are golden brown on all sides. Remove from the oil with a slotted spoon and place on a plate lined with kitchen paper (paper towels) to drain any excess oil and cool slightly.

Best served and enjoyed immediately.

Festivals

A festival is a thing of beauty. It jumps into that sweet-and-savoury at the same time spot that I just adore. The first time I had one of these was in Montego Bay, with a plate of hot smoky BBQ, and I can confirm bliss was achieved. Put them on your summertime menu! (Put them on your anytime menu.)

250g (1⅔ cups) fine cornmeal (polenta)

450g (scant 3½ cups) plain (all-purpose) flour, plus extra for handling dough

6 tbsp brown or granulated white sugar

2 tsp baking powder

3 tbsp softened unsalted butter or margarine

1 tsp vanilla extract

1 tsp ground allspice or nutmeg

1 tsp salt

240ml (1 cup) cold full-fat milk (sweetened or unsweetened), or water, plus an extra splash if needed

neutral oil, such as rapeseed (canola) or sunflower oil, for frying

Makes 16
Prep time 15 minutes, plus 35 minutes resting time
Cook time 15 minutes

Combine the cornmeal, flour, sugar, baking powder, butter, vanilla extract, allspice or nutmeg, and salt in a large mixing bowl. Slowly add the milk or water, mixing to bring all the ingredients together until a manageable dough forms. Cover the bowl with cling film (plastic wrap) or a damp kitchen towel and rest the dough at room temperature for 35 minutes.

Heat the oil in a deep-fat fryer or heavy-based saucepan to 170°C (340°F).

Meanwhile, place the dough onto a well-floured work surface. Knead the dough into a ball and, using well-floured hands, pinch and divide the dough into 16 equal portions. Roll each portion into a long cigar/sausage-like shape with slightly tapered ends.

To test whether the oil is hot enough, drop a piece of dough into the oil. If it bubbles straight away and goes golden, then the oil is ready for frying. Gently slip 3–4 festivals into the hot oil and fry for about 4 minutes on each side until perfectly golden brown all over. Remove from the oil with a slotted spoon and place on a plate lined with kitchen paper (paper towels) to drain any excess oil. Repeat the frying process with the remaining dough. Best served and enjoyed immediately.

Note to reader
Supposedly named after the Jamaica festival of Arts and Culture – as well as the nature of their consumption being "as fun as a festival" – festivals, fried dumplings, and many of their other Caribbean counterparts have origins in colonization and slavery, where it is said workers prepared and stored these simple yet high carb, calorie-dense snacks for long journeys. Also known as cornbread fritters or fried cornbread, festivals are a street food traditionally served alongside fry fish and escovitch pickle and jerk seasoned meats.

Coco bread

Makes 8–10
Prep time 20 minutes, plus 1–2 hours resting time
Cook time 15–20 minutes

Not, as some assume, named after chocolate, but actually presumably for the somewhat unusual inclusion of coconut milk, coco bread is said to have come about due to the scarcity of ingredients experienced, and subsequent innovation employed by enslaved and colonized peoples.

Today it has become a staple in Jamaican cuisine, often served alongside stews and soups as a sort of dinner roll, or filled with cheese and/or a patty (we LOVE a double and even sometimes a triple carb!) as a serious snack. The robust, rich dough means it makes the perfect sandwich, and it's easy to make it an ital marvel (see page 156). I like to think of it as a kind of Caribbean brioche – you can stuff these breads with anything you fancy – barbecued chicken, fried fish, crispy mushrooms, bacon and egg... it ALL works!

110g (scant ½ cup) unsalted butter
    or coconut oil, melted

250ml (1 cup plus 1 tbsp) coconut milk,
    full-fat dairy milk or water

3 tbsp caster (granulated) sugar

1 tsp salt

2½ tsp instant dried yeast

1 UK large (US extra-large) egg, lightly beaten

450g (scant 3½ cups) plain (all-purpose)
    flour, plus extra for dusting

Line a large baking tray with baking parchment. Lightly grease a large bowl and the lined baking tray with a small amount of the melted butter or oil and set aside.

Add the coconut milk, milk, or water, most of the remaining melted butter or oil (reserve a small amount for brushing) and the sugar and salt to a saucepan. Warm through gently over a very low heat, stirring until the sugar has dissolved and the ingredients have combined, being careful not to let the mixture boil or get too hot. Remove the pan from the heat and stir in the yeast and egg. Add the flour and stir together lightly to form a slightly sticky dough.

Turn the dough out onto a lightly floured work surface – try not to add too much extra flour as a softer dough will result in a more delicate final product. Knead for about 4–8 minutes until the dough is slightly firmer, yet soft and smooth.

Place the dough into the greased bowl and coat the dough in a little more butter or oil to avoid sticking. Cover with a damp kitchen towel and leave to rest in a warm place for 1–2 hours, or until the dough has roughly doubled in size.

Preheat the oven to 175°C fan (195°C/380°F/Gas 5).

Once the dough has risen, punch it down in the bowl, then tip out onto a lightly floured work surface and cut into 8–10 equal portions.

Roll each portion into a ball, then use a rolling pin to gently roll the balls into flat oval-like shapes (about 15cm/6in wide and 1.5cm/⅝in thick). Brush the surface of each oval with butter or oil, then fold in half to form a semi-circle. Brush the tops again with the remaining butter or oil and place on the prepared baking tray. Leave to rest at room temperature for 10–15 minutes until slightly risen again.

Bake in the preheated oven for 12–15 minutes until lightly golden brown.

Dhal puri roti

Makes 12
Prep time 30 minutes, plus 35–55 minutes
resting time
Cook time 50 minutes

Puri are another manifestation of the Indian hand in Caribbean cooking. This golden cousin of the roti is stuffed with deeply spiced yellow split peas. A puri is satisfying, delicious and decidedly moreish... I mean, who doesn't like flaky golden stuffed bread??

For the filling

250g (generous 1⅓ cups) yellow split peas, soaked overnight

3 tsp finely grated garlic

2 tbsp finely grated onion

1 tsp very finely chopped Scotch bonnet or other chilli of your choice or chilli flakes

2 tsp cumin seeds or ground cumin

1 tbsp finely chopped coriander (cilantro)

For the dough

350g (2¾ cups) plain (all-purpose) flour, plus extra for dusting

1 tsp white sugar

1–2 tsp salt, to taste, plus extra for seasoning

1 tsp baking powder

1½ tbsp ghee or oil, plus extra for greasing and cooking

300–400ml (1¼–1¾ cups) lukewarm water

food processor

To make the filling, drain and rinse the soaked yellow split peas. Add the split peas to a large saucepan with 1.5 litres (6¼ cups) of salted water and bring to the boil. Cook for about 30 minutes until just tender but still with a little bite.

Drain well, then spread the split peas out on a wide, flat surface to cool. Once cooled, combine the split peas in a food processor with the garlic, onion, chilli, cumin, and coriander and pulse to a rough consistency. Set aside.

For the dough, combine the flour, sugar, salt, and baking powder in a large mixing bowl. Add the ghee or oil and combine using your hand or a wooden spoon. Gradually add 300ml (1¼ cups) of the lukewarm water, mixing until a soft dough comes together. You may or may not need to add the extra 100ml (generous ⅓ cup) to bring it all together.

Transfer the dough to a lightly floured work surface and knead for around 5 minutes until the dough is soft and elastic. Grease the dough with 1 teaspoon of ghee or oil. Cover with a damp kitchen towel and leave to rest at room temperature for at least 15 minutes and up to 30 minutes.

Divide the dough into 12 equal portions and roll into balls. Cover again and leave to rest for another 10–15 minutes.

Gently flatten each portioned dough ball using a rolling pin or your hand and lightly dust with flour. Place 1–2 teaspoons of the split pea mixture into the centre of each dough round and pinch the dough closed around the filling to form balls again. Cover and leave to rest at room temperature again for a further 10 minutes.

Once finally rested, heat a heavy-based frying pan, cast iron skillet, or traditional griddle (tawah) over a medium heat. Use a rolling pin to gently roll the dough balls out into even, thin circles (about 3–4mm/⅛in thick). Gently transfer a dough round to the hot pan and brush with some ghee or oil. Quickly flip over and brush with more ghee or oil on the other side. Cook the puri on each side until tender, slightly puffy and covered in golden brown spots. Repeat the cooking process for the remaining dough.

Best served and enjoyed immediately.

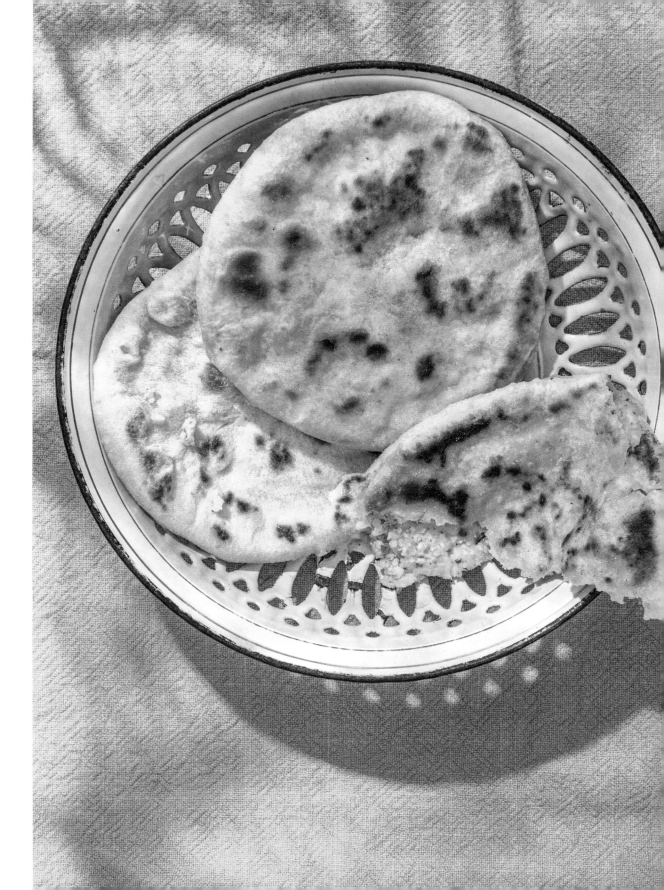

Duff

Makes 5–8
Prep time 15 minutes, plus 20–30 minutes resting time
Cook time 15 minutes

Ooh, duff! Fluffy clouds of gently steamed dumplings, most often seen as an accompaniment to the Guyanese metemgee (a delicious coconut stew made with ground provision/root vegetables), but also served on the side of a plate of saltfish or any other stew situation you desire... soothing, comforting and just wonderful.

300g (2¼ cups) plain (all-purpose) flour

1½ tsp baking powder

3½ tbsp brown sugar, golden sugar or coconut sugar

small pinch of salt

1½ tbsp unsalted butter, softened

200–250ml (scant 1 cup–1 cup plus 1 tbsp) warm water (about 37–43°C/98–109°F)

In a large mixing bowl, combine the flour, baking powder, sugar, and salt. Add the softened butter and stir well with a wooden spoon until evenly combined. Form a well in the centre of the dry mixture and begin to slowly add 200ml (scant 1 cup) of the warm water, stirring together until a dough forms. You may or may not need to add the extra 50ml (1⅔fl oz) water to bring it all together.

Knead the dough in the bowl for 2 minutes or so until soft and smooth, being careful not to overwork it to ensure it stays delicate. Cover the bowl with a damp kitchen towel and leave to rest at room temperature for a minimum of 20 and up to 30 minutes.

Once rested and ready to cook, divide the dough into 5–8 equal portions and roll into little oval shapes.

You can steam the dumplings in a few different ways. Traditionally, they are steamed over a rich ground provision and coconut stew known as metemgee, but the simplest option is to use a shallow pot of boiling water with a tight lid, or you can even use a steamer basket. Prepare your chosen steamer and steam the dumplings for around 15 minutes, making sure to leave the lid on whilst they are cooking to achieve the best results. Remove immediately from the heat and serve.

Johnny cakes

Makes 8–12
Prep time 15 minutes, plus 10–20 minutes resting time
Cook time 20–30 minutes

Johnny cakes, also known as bakes or fry bakes, are found in Antigua and across many of the smaller Caribbean isles. They are synonymous with Trinidad and Tobago floats or Jamaican fried dumplings. Antiguan Johnny cakes, however, differ slightly from their counterparts in that they are generally shallow-fried, smaller, include sugar and have a distinct lack of yeast.

Story has it that the name is derived from "journey cake". The easy nature of their construction means that they could be whipped up quickly, ready to be stuffed into a pocket or bag to provide sustenance for long days of hard field work or travel.

Nowadays, they are an Antiguan staple. I grew up eating Johnny cakes, and they are my favourite iteration of the fried dumpling. My cousin, Gerry, actually calls my mum the Johnny Cake Lady, and there is much discussion in the family as to whose Johnny cakes are the best. I am going to remain loyal and tell you that no one else's taste quite like my mum's!!

470g (3½ cups) plain (all-purpose) flour, plus extra for dusting

2 tsp baking powder

2 tsp white sugar

big pinch of salt

4 tbsp room temperature unsalted butter or plant-based alternative of your choice

about 300–600ml (1½–2½ cups) neutral oil, such as rapeseed (canola) or sunflower oil, for shallow-frying

Combine the flour, baking powder, sugar, and salt in a large mixing bowl. Add the butter (or fat of your choice). Begin to add 250ml (1 cup plus 1 tbsp) water, a little at a time, bringing the mixture together with your hands until a dough starts to form. Turn the dough out onto a lightly floured work surface and knead gently until it becomes smooth with a bit of elasticity. Dust with a little more flour if the dough gets too sticky. Return the dough to the bowl, cover with a damp kitchen towel and leave to rest at room temperature for at least 10 minutes and up to 20 minutes.

Heat the oil in a heavy-based, deep saucepan to 180°C (350°F).

Pinch and divide the dough into 8–12 equal portions and roll into balls. Slightly flatten each dough ball using your hand, then slip into the hot oil. Just fry a few at a time as you don't want to overcrowd the pan. Leave the cakes to cook for a few minutes on each side, turning as they become golden underneath. Once they are evenly golden brown all over, remove from the oil with a slotted spoon and place on a plate lined with kitchen paper (paper towels) to drain any excess oil. Repeat the frying process with the remaining dough.

Best served and enjoyed immediately, usually alongside curry or an Antiguan breakfast.

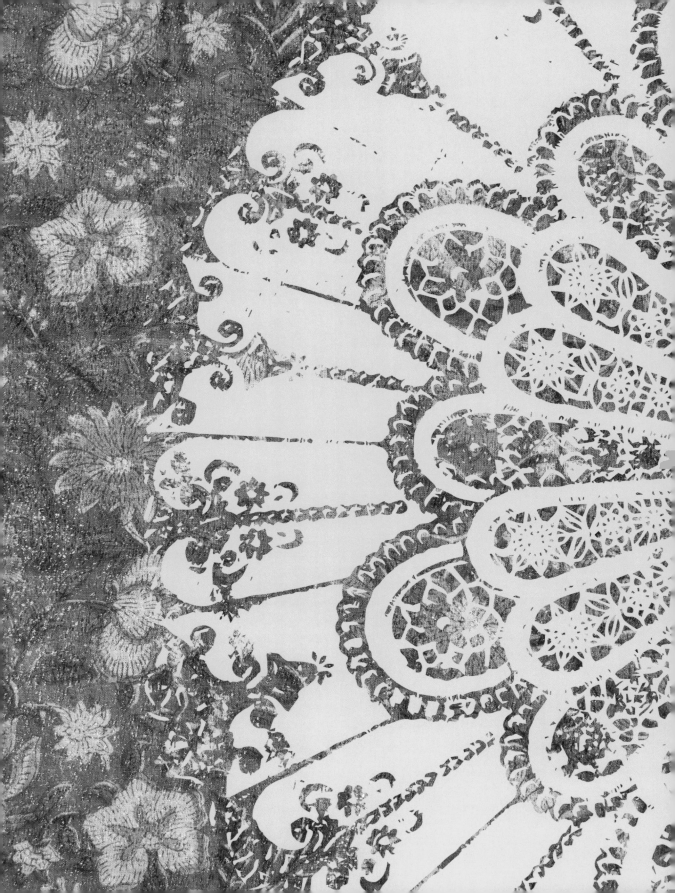

Rice & also peas

You can't even imagine Caribbean food without rice. It's more than a staple, it's home on a plate. It's heart, it's soul… it's the core of the volcano and the pull of the ocean wave.

It's difficult to split this particular ingredient up into regional specialities, because pretty much everyone makes the same stuff with their rice. For instance, Trinidadians call theirs pelau, but it is essentially the same as season rice, which is made in Jamaica and Antigua, and a whole bunch of other islands, and EVERYONE MAKES RICE AND PEAS!

When we refer to peas, we actually mean beans. And the variety of peas that are used differs from house to house, or moment to moment, depending on what is chosen that day. There are red peas, black-eyed peas, gungo peas (which some call pigeon peas), black beans, pinto beans, navy beans… you get the picture.

Sometimes rice and peas is made with coconut milk or coconut water, sometimes with stock, sometimes just with salted water. Rather than this choice differing from island to island, it's more about what you and your family like to do.

I feel like, for us, rice and peas are such good friends that to split them up would feel wrong. So in this chapter, we will explore both. Here we go!

Saturday 19th January

Mum & Jeannette

One of my dearest friends in the entire world, Jeannette, has just arrived. Some people in life just feel like home. She is Miquita's godmother and one of the best human beings I know.

When we were young, we would spend a lot of time lying around together in a huge (HUGE) bed in our friend Vivien Goldman's house, laughing, laughing, laughing. We both dreamed about a future life in which we would each become the mistress of our own destiny and be free to do the things we love... and finally, here we are!

For years now, Jeannette has run a legendary independent record label called Rough Trade, and she is responsible for the careers of some of the most outstanding artists of our generation. She is like a finely tuned instrument with an extraordinary ear for music that hears beyond the surface and the superficial, and I am so proud of her. I am cooking, reading, and writing and doing all the things I always dreamt of. We survived and now we thrive.

We have talked about making this trip and being here in Antigua together for 35 years, and it has miraculously and suddenly just happened! Jeannette is my family, and yes, it bears repeating, when we're together it feels like being home. When we were young and skint, SO SKINT, I used to cook for us all the time. I've only just realized that I often used to cook Jeannette things that my mum made for me, without thinking this was probably because I was missing mum and missing her food. Jeannette being here has sparked daydreams of the lovely food Mum used to make.

My mother is an extraordinary woman. She's smart, brave, stylish, patient, beautiful, and funny, with the heart of a lioness. So much of what forms the heart of me, the basis of who I am, comes from my mum. She took me to the library every week when I was a kid and instilled in me a lifesaving love of books. Mum, my brother Sean and I, used to lie on our backs and chart the stars in the night sky when we lived in Cyprus. She taught us the names of trees and flowers and spices and, most importantly, she taught us to be brave and to be kind. These life lessons have supported me through thick and thin, they're the reason I'm still here. She is the reason I'm still here. Thank you, Mum, for everything, always.

She's funny about her own cooking, my mum. She thinks she can't cook, but much of what I know about cooking deep down, I learnt from both her AND my dad. There is just something about your mum's cooking, it's more than just the food itself, it carries the potent combination of care, safety, and familiarity (if you're lucky, of course!). Sometimes, it's all you need.

There is an expression in the Caribbean that says you like someone's "hand", which means that you like the invisible things that they imbue a dish with. My mum makes the best rice, the kids call it "nanny rice", and sometimes it's all I crave. I used to make versions of it for me and Jeannette all the time. The broader term in Antiguan cooking for our nanny rice is "season rice". It can be a "use what's in the fridge and going a bit moody" kind of dish – which I'm always a big fan of, or you can decide exactly which delights you're going to sexy it up with, and be very deliberate about it. There's something about it that I've always found to be exceedingly soothing and comforting.

When I think about it, this kind of rice happens all over the world in one way or another. There's jollof, pilaf, pelau, biriyani, risotto, paella... you get the picture. And in Antigua, there is season rice. Tonight, I've come up with this version that's somewhat fancier than we would have had when I was a kid, but it still has the ability to quiet the troubled mind and to soothe the restless spirit. AND, I've made smoked chilli syrup and bathed some chicken wings in it after roasting them slowly in the oven. Delicious!

ON THE MENU TODAY

COLA-BRAISED SHORT RIB
SPINACH SEASON RICE

GINGER BEER

SMOKED CHILLI SYRUP-
DRENCHED CHICKEN WINGS

Cola-braised short rib spinach season rice

Cooking with cola is something I discovered reading that seminal and most brilliant of cookbooks, *White Trash Cooking* by Ernest Matthew Mickler. The soda caramelizes and helps to deliver a wonderful, bittersweet flavour along with the spinach season rice.

Serves 6–8
Prep time 25 minutes
Cook time about 5 hours

3½ tbsp rapeseed (canola) oil

1 large onion, thinly sliced

5 garlic cloves, finely grated

3 bird's-eye chillies (see Note to reader), finely chopped

620g (1lb 6oz) beef short ribs, seasoned

500ml (generous 2 cups) cola

2 tbsp blackstrap molasses or treacle

2 tbsp dark soy sauce

For the season rice

splash of rapeseed (canola) oil

1 large onion, thinly sliced

2 garlic cloves, grated

1½ tbsp unsalted butter

450g (2½ cups) jasmine rice

reserved cooking liquid from the short ribs

300ml (1¼ cups) chicken stock

300g (10½oz) spinach

salt (optional)

store-bought crispy onions, to garnish

Preheat the oven to 200°C fan (220°C/425°F/Gas 7).

Heat half the oil in a frying pan and gently sauté the onions, garlic, and chillies over a low heat for 10 minutes until soft. Remove from the pan and transfer to a roasting tray.

Add the remaining oil to the frying pan and let it heat up for a couple of minutes. Slip the seasoned short ribs into the pan and let them caramelize on each side until they have a little crust. Remove from the pan and add to the roasting tray on top of the onions, garlic, and chillies.

Combine the cola, molasses or treacle, and soy sauce in a jug or cup and give it a mix to bring everything together. Pour this over the short ribs in the tray. Cover the tray with a sheet of baking parchment, then a sheet of tin foil and slip into the preheated oven for 3½–4 hours until meltingly tender.

Remove the ribs from the liquor (keep this precious nectar for the spinach season rice). Cool, then pull the meat from the bone. Chop the meat and leave to one side.

To make the spinach season rice, pour the rapeseed (canola) oil into a heavy-based saucepan over a low heat. Add the onion and garlic and cook for 5 minutes until softened. Add the butter and let it melt before adding the rice. Stir through so that all the grains are coated in melted butter.

Add the chopped rib meat to the pan of rice, then pour in the short rib cooking liquid and chicken stock. Check the seasoning – you may want to add a dash more salt at this point, but be careful because the cooking liquid has already been seasoned. Cover the pan with a lid and leave over a low heat for around 50–60 minutes, until all the grains of rice are tender and nearly all the liquid has been absorbed.

Remove the lid and lay all the spinach on top of the rice. Replace the lid and leave for another 10 minutes. Remove the lid again; the spinach should be wilting by now, so stir it through the rice until it is broken down and soft.

Remove from the heat and leave to stand and rest for 5 minutes. Top the rice with a scattering of crispy onions and serve.

Note to reader

If you don't like it hot, just use one or two bird's-eye chillies or a chilli of your choice instead. For a mild-to-medium heat, use a couple of long red or green chillies. For a blast of fiery heat use Scotch bonnet, but just the one!

Ginger beer

Makes 2 litres (8½ cups)
Prep time 10 minutes, plus steeping time
Cook time 5 minutes

Mum's recipe for ginger beer is so simple, refreshing, and wonderful. I've been drinking this all my life. Just add a dash of rum for fun!

500g (1lb 2oz) fresh ginger, peeled and grated

1 large or 2 small cinnamon sticks

1 tsp vanilla extract or 1 vanilla pod, split down the middle

maple syrup, agave syrup, or a simple sugar syrup, to taste

juice of a lime

1 tbsp rum or rum essence (optional)

Add the grated ginger to a large pot with the cinnamon stick(s), vanilla, and 2 litres (8½ cups) water.

Simmer over a medium–low heat for 5 minutes (keeping the heat fairly low will ensure the ginger warms through without cooking it or destroying the flavour).

Remove the pot from the stove and add your sweetener of choice. Let the liquid cool, then add the lime juice.

Cover the pot and store in a cool place or in the fridge for at least several hours or up to a week (the longer you leave it to rest the stronger it will taste).

When you are ready to serve, strain the liquid through a muslin (cheesecloth) or an extra-fine mesh sieve. This is the moment to add the rum or rum essence (if using). Add more water if it's too strong and/or adjust the sweetener to your taste.

Serve over ice. You can add fizzy water if it takes your fancy.

Smoked chilli syrup-drenched chicken wings

I love a chicken wing. Any which way you want to give them to me, I'm here for it. This version is sticky, smoky, hot with spicy pepper, and a brilliant but inexpensive way to make a wing royal.

Serves 4–6

Prep time 15 minutes, plus overnight marination and soaking time

Cook time 1 hour 45 minutes–2 hours 15 minutes

150ml (⅔ cup) Smoked Chilli Syrup (see recipe, right)

2kg (4½lb) chicken wings

2 onions, finely chopped

6 garlic cloves, crushed

thumb-size piece of fresh ginger, peeled and grated

handful of parsley, finely chopped

handful of coriander (cilantro), finely chopped, plus extra to serve

juice of 2 limes

juice of 2 lemons

juice of 2 oranges

1 Scotch bonnet, finely chopped

4 tbsp soy sauce or tamari

1 tsp ground cumin

1 tsp ground coriander

1 tsp ground allspice

good pinch of thyme leaves, picked and finely chopped

1 tbsp English mustard or mustard of your choice

5 tbsp dark or golden rum

1 tbsp freshly ground black pepper

1 tbsp ground sea salt

2 tbsp olive oil

handful of thinly sliced red chilli, to serve

handful of thinly sliced spring onions (scallions), to serve

For the smoked chilli syrup

500ml (generous 2 cups) boiled water, cooled slightly

40g (1½oz) cascabel chillies or other smoked dried chillies of your choice

500g (2½ cups) white sugar

airtight bottle or jar

Start by making the smoked chilli syrup. Pour the warm water over the chillies in a large heatproof bowl and leave to steep for about 1 hour until they are soft.

Remove the chillies from the water (reserving the water) and finely chop them. Add the chillies to a saucepan with the soaking water and the sugar. Set the pan over a medium–low heat for around 30 minutes, until the sugar has melted and is bubbling into a syrup. Leave to cool, then transfer to an airtight bottle or jar and keep in the fridge. This recipe makes more than you need for the wings (about 550ml/2⅓ cups in total), but the tasty leftovers will keep for up to 2–3 weeks.

Cut the chicken wings in half. Wash the chicken in a solution made with water and a splash of lemon juice or white vinegar. This step is optional, but it is considered key in Caribbean culture. Pat the meat dry with kitchen paper (paper towels).

Place the chicken wings and all the remaining ingredients, apart from the smoked chilli syrup, into a bowl and mix well. Cover with cling film (plastic wrap) and leave to marinate in the fridge for at least 1 hour, or preferably overnight.

When you are ready to cook, preheat the oven to 150°C fan (170°C/340°F/Gas 4).

Transfer the chicken wings to a large roasting tray, discarding any leftover marinade, as this has now done its job. Roast the chicken wings in the middle of the preheated oven for around 60–90 minutes. Check them every 20 minutes, turning the wings to make sure they are cooking evenly. When the chicken skin is golden all over, the juices are running clear, and the meat is soft they are cooked.

Crank up the oven temperature to 180°C fan (200°C/400°F/Gas 6). Drizzle the smoked chilli syrup over the wings and roast for a further 15 minutes until they are beautifully caramelized. Serve on a big platter with a scattering of sliced red chilli and spring onions (scallions).

Red pea soup

Serves 6–8
Prep time 25 minutes, plus overnight soaking time
Cook time 3 hours 20 minutes

One-pot dishes like this live at the very heart of Caribbean cooking, and they make a little go a very long way. This recipe is deeply satisfying, and a mainstay at large gatherings. For instance, if you go to a Caribbean funeral, you'll probably be given a cup of red pea soup when you get there before all the other food is brought out. It keeps the wolves from the door, is fully rounded and calms the mind and the body.

400g (2¼ cups) dried red peas

900g (2lb) salted pig tails, chopped into small pieces (a butcher can do this for you)

1 onion, roughly chopped

1 large carrot, roughly chopped

1 whole Scotch bonnet (or use 2 roughly chopped bird's-eye chillies)

4 garlic cloves, roughly chopped

4 sprigs of thyme

1 sprig of marjoram (optional)

2 bay leaves

1 teaspoon ground black pepper

1 tsp allspice berries

1 cinnamon stick

1 x 400ml (13.5fl oz) can coconut milk

2 white sweet potatoes, diced

100g (3½oz) pumpkin, peeled, deseeded, and finely diced

salt, to taste

2 spring onions (scallions), to garnish

For the dropper dumplings

200g (1½ cups) self-raising flour

salt, to taste

Soak the red peas in a deep bowl of cold water overnight. At the same time, add the pig tails to a separate deep pot with enough cold water to cover. Bring to the boil for 10 minutes, then drain and repeat the boiling process with fresh water. This process removes the salt from the tails and makes them tender. Leave the pig tails to cool, then transfer to a covered container and leave in the fridge overnight.

The next day, drain the red peas. Take a heavy-based, very deep saucepan and add the red peas, onion, carrot, chillies, garlic, all the herbs, black pepper (not the salt), allspice berries, cinnamon stick, and enough water to generously cover. Bring to a vigorous boil over a high heat. As it comes up to boil, skim off and discard any froth that floats to the top. Turn the heat down to medium–low and simmer for an hour, or until the peas are becoming tender. Keep the water in the pot topped up to the same high level all the while.

Add the pig tails and cook for another 1 hour 30 minutes, until they are soft. You can test the pig tails by spooning a couple out and squeezing them between your fingers – you should be able to squash them with no resistance. If they are not there, just top up the pan with a little more water and try them again after another 30 minutes of cooking.

Add the coconut milk, sweet potatoes, and pumpkin. At this point, the liquid in the pot should have reduced to a level just above the peas and vegetables; if it's lower than this, just add a splash more water. Leave to bubble for around 40 minutes until the vegetables are cooked through. Adjust the seasoning with more salt to taste.

Now make your dropper dumplings. Combine the flour with a pinch of salt and about 250ml (1 cup plus 1 tablespoon) cold water in a bowl until you have a slightly sticky dough. Pinch off a small amount of dough at a time (about 1 tablespoon) and roll it into a long shape resembling a cigar. Drop the dumplings into the soup and turn up the heat to medium–high. Simmer for around 10 minutes and the dumplings will float to the top of the pan and roll as they cook through. Serve hot.

Pelau

Oooh pelau... it's just a comfort in any storm.
Chicken (or whatever meat you choose) is
simmered down in fluffy, perfect rice. A hint
of sweetness, barely shimmering through
the background, makes this dish glorious.

Serves 8
Prep time 20 minutes, plus marinating time
Cook time about 1 hour

500g (1lb 2oz) chicken thighs and
    drumsticks, skin on and bone in

4 tbsp Green Seasoning (see page 110)

2 tbsp soy sauce

1 tbsp Worcestershire sauce

3 tbsp ghee, unsalted butter, or coconut oil

2 tbsp light or dark brown sugar

1 medium–large onion, thinly sliced

1 tbsp finely grated garlic

1 tbsp finely grated fresh ginger

1 celery stick, finely diced

1 carrot, finely diced

125g (4½oz) dried gungo peas (pigeon peas),
    soaked overnight and pre-cooked (see
    Note to reader), or 1 x 400g (14oz) can of
    cooked gungo peas, drained and rinsed

2 sprigs of thyme

2 bay leaves

1–2 tsp minced Scotch bonnet or fresh red
    or green hot chilli, to your taste

3 spring onions (scallions), thinly sliced

1 tbsp tomato purée (tomato paste)

1 tbsp Caribbean browning sauce

1 tsp ground cumin

2 cinnamon sticks

1 x 400ml (13.5fl oz) can of coconut milk

250ml (1 cup plus 1 tbsp) chicken stock

500g (1lb 2oz) basmati or jasmine rice

200g (7oz) pumpkin or butternut squash,
    peeled, deseeded, and diced

1 tbsp finishing butter, such as Green
    Seasoning Butter (see page 111)

2 tbsp chopped parsley

2 tbsp chopped coriander (cilantro)

salt and freshly ground black pepper

Wash the chicken in a solution made with water and a splash of lemon juice or white vinegar. This step is entirely optional, but it is considered key in Caribbean culture. Pat the meat dry with kitchen paper (paper towels).

Place the chicken pieces in a deep bowl. Add 2 tablespoons of the green seasoning, the soy sauce, and Worcestershire sauce. Mix well to coat the chicken in the marinade. Cover the bowl with cling film (plastic wrap) and leave in the fridge to marinate for a minimum of 30 minutes (even better if you can give it a few hours or overnight if you have time).

Warm a large saucepan or casserole dish over a medium–high heat and add the ghee, butter, or oil. Now turn the heat down low and add the sugar. Let it gently melt and caramelize, taking care that it doesn't burn. Once the sugar is brown and bubbling, immediately stir in the marinated chicken pieces and cook until coated in sugar and browned all over; this will take around 15 minutes.

Add the onion, garlic, ginger, celery, and carrot and let them soften for a couple of minutes.

Add a small splash of water to stop anything sticking, then cover the pan and simmer for about 5–10 minutes.

Next, add the cooked gungo peas, thyme, bay leaves, chilli, spring onions (scallions), remaining green seasoning, tomato purée, browning sauce, cumin, and cinnamon sticks.

Give it a good stir, then add the coconut milk, chicken stock, 250ml (1 cup plus 1 tablespoon) of water, the rice, and diced pumpkin or squash. Season with the salt and pepper. Put the lid back on again and gently simmer for about 25–30 minutes, or until most of the liquid has evaporated and the rice and vegetables are tender.

Remove from the heat and fluff the rice with a fork. Stir in the finishing butter, then garnish with parsley and coriander (cilantro). Serve hot – although I also like it cold... any which way is delicious.

Note to reader

If you are cooking dried gungo peas in advance, add the soaked peas to a deep pan (along with any flavourings you fancy such as a halved onion, garlic cloves, allspice, thyme, etc.). Cover the peas with 1.5 litres (6¼ cups) of water, then bring to the boil over a high heat. Turn the heat down and simmer gently for about 35–40 minutes. After this time, the water will be greatly reduced, with a just a little left in the pot. Most importantly, the peas should be so tender that when you squeeze one between your fingers it smooshes easily (technical term). If the water is reduced but they're still not soft, then add another 200ml (scant 1 cup) or so of water and simmer for longer until the gungo peas are tender.

Coconut rice

Serves 4–6
Prep time 10 minutes
Cook time 25–35 minutes

Coconut and rice are, of course, a match made in heaven, which is why so many cultures make a version of this dish.

2 tbsp unsalted butter

1 onion or shallot, finely diced

1 small garlic clove, grated

4 tbsp unsweetened creamed coconut purée/coconut cream, or use 125ml (½ cup) good-quality coconut milk

450g (2½ cups) long-grain jasmine rice, or rice of your choice

1 sprig of thyme

½ tsp ground allspice

800ml (3⅓ cups) light chicken stock, or water

1–2 fresh bay leaves

1 tsp salt

1 tsp fresh cracked black pepper or ground white pepper

2–4 tbsp toasted coconut flakes (optional), to serve

1–2 spring onions (scallions), thinly sliced, to serve

Gently melt the butter in a heavy-based saucepan over a low heat. Add the onion and garlic and lightly sauté for about 5 minutes until fragrant, being careful not to brown the butter or let any of the other ingredients brown.

Add the creamed coconut/coconut cream or milk, rice, thyme, and ground allspice. Gently stir the rice into the coconut mixture to evenly coat all the grains. Add the chicken stock or water, bay leaves, and salt and pepper. Cover the pan and cook over a very low heat for about 20–30 minutes until the liquids have been absorbed and the rice is fluffy and tender.

Once cooked, fluff the rice up gently. Stir in half of the toasted coconut (if using) and garnish with the remaining toasted coconut and spring onions (scallions). Best served immediately alongside a curry or stew of your choice.

Quick chana dhal

Serves 6–8
Prep time 15 minutes
Cook time 33–38 minutes

Chana means chickpea. This dish has a direct and clear link to its southern Indian origins. It's a robust curry, redolent with cumin and smoky spices. This version is simple, quick, and wonderfully versatile.

1 onion, chopped

4 garlic cloves, peeled

1 long red chilli

1 tsp ground cumin

1 tsp ground coriander

1 tsp ground turmeric

2 tsp Caribbean curry powder

4 tbsp neutral oil, such as rapeseed (canola) or sunflower oil

big pinch of salt

1 tsp whole cumin seeds

1 tsp green cardamom pods

1 tsp split mustard seeds (optional)

2 x 400g (14oz) cans of chickpeas, drained

300ml (1¼ cups) vegetable or chicken stock

200ml (scant 1 cup) coconut milk

2 tbsp Green Seasoning (see page 110)

food processor

In a food processor, blitz together the onion, garlic cloves, chilli, ground cumin, coriander, turmeric, curry powder, and 2 tablespoons of the oil to a rough paste.

Heat the remaining 2 tablespoons of oil in a large pan over a medium heat. Add the curry paste and salt and sauté gently for about 5 minutes, giving it a light stir occasionally.

Now add the whole cumin seeds, green cardamom pods, and mustard seeds (if using). Stir the mixture around while cooking for another 3 minutes.

Add the drained chickpeas and give everything a good stir until thoroughly combined. Pour in the stock, add the green seasoning and coconut milk and simmer gently over a low heat for 20–25 minutes, until the sauce is thickened and delicious. Serve.

Rice & peas

Serves 8
Prep time 10 minutes, plus overnight soaking
Cook time 1 hour 30 minutes

This is possibly THE most famous Caribbean dish of all. One bite of it sends me careering back through my life, memories of family parties, both as a girl waiting to be fed, and as a grown woman waiting for the rice and peas to be done so that I could in my turn do the feeding of the throng. In some ways, it's the backbone of a Caribbean celebration table, but also a pot that you'd find in kitchens any day of the week. It's all and everything, and I can't imagine life without this dish. Made right across the region, each household will have its own particular recipe.

500g (3 cups) dried black-eyed beans (black-eyed peas), soaked overnight

½ onion, peeled

3 garlic cloves, peeled and smashed

1 tsp whole allspice berries

small handful of thyme

300g (1⅔ cups) basmati or jasmine rice

1 x 400ml (13.5fl oz) can of coconut milk

150ml (⅔ cup) chicken or vegetable stock

salt

Drain the soaked black-eyed beans and place them in a deep saucepan with the onion, garlic, allspice, thyme, and 1.5 litres (6¼ cups) of fresh cold water. Bring to the boil over a high heat, then turn the heat down and simmer gently for about 35–40 minutes.

By now the water will be greatly reduced, with a just a little left in the pot. Most importantly, the beans should be tender enough that if you squeeze one between your fingers it smooshes easily (technical term). If the water has reduced but the beans still aren't soft, just add another 200ml (scant 1 cup) or so of water and simmer again until they are tender.

Next, add the rice, coconut milk, stock, and 2–3 good big pinches of salt. Leave the heat low, cover the pot and let it cook out for a further 40 minutes, until all the liquid has been absorbed and the rice is fluffy. Serve hot.

Curries in the Caribbean

Alright, quick bit of cursory history here. Although these days "curry" is synonymous with Caribbean cooking, it actually didn't really arrive until the mid-1800s, after emancipation.

The British hauled hundreds of indentured labourers from all over Pakistan, Bangladesh, Sri Lanka, India, and beyond to replace some of the labour that was lost on the plantations. They brought not only their tired bodies to join ours, but also their exceptional food. These new techniques, flavours, and textures inevitably made their way into Caribbean cuisine, and they have since become a staple of our culinary lexicon – here endeth your (very brief) history lesson!

Curries and the spices that make them sing are now everywhere in our food. The magic application of a little allspice here, a little cumin there, a hint of chilli or a pop of coriander is, for me, what makes the world turn. This is another scenario where it's not truly possible to attribute one dish to one island, so we're just going to explore all my favourites.

Curry goat, curry chicken, curry shrimp, curry crab, and on we go.

Sunday 17th January

The Great House

We've been invited to go to a hotel in the north-east of the island called The Great House. The name implied it could be an old sugar plantation, and it is indeed that. A stunning house set on the top of a hill with a picturesque aspect and views over acres of lush verdant land, all tumbling down into the crystal turquoise ocean. It's an undeniably beautiful scene.

As we roll up the drive, the gorgeous house looms into view and I get a sick feeling in my stomach. I feel the long shadows cast by the past. The ghosts of the enslaved Africans who were dragged here are swirling all around. I imagine how terrible it must have been to arrive at this place, shackled and beaten and frightened. I look to the left and see the old sugar mill, it's crumbling now but somehow I feel it's still held up in part by the black bodies that built and sustained it and its bloody crop back in its working days. We're greeted at the door by the loveliest woman who ushers us to our table. We ooh and ahh, because it's a stunning place, and we do so too as we pass an old heavy black iron bell. What was it used for I wonder? To signal to the tired, broken bodies that they must get up and start the tortuous day all over again? It brings tears to my throat, an inescapable sadness from the heavy weight of the history.

The house itself is incredibly handsome, and we discover that it's built from Bath stone. That's why it's oddly familiar. I know that stone, that design. I know that part of England quite well. The ships would take sugar to Bristol and collect enslaved people and stones to bring back, to build antebellum houses just like this one. I am struck by the thought that so much horror and torture has historically been perpetrated in the most beautiful of settings. A most terrible juxtaposition.

I have a feeling of needing to stand tall for those that have come before us, our elders. A feeling that this is our NOW and that, whatever we do, we shall carry them with us in our hearts, pull our shoulders back and be proud that their blood runs through us and that we can give them voice and spirit. I think of the amazing and inspirational black chef, Mashama Bailey, who runs a restaurant called The Grey in Savannah, deep in southern America. It's in an old, segregated bus station, a place where her forebears would not even have been able to set foot. The image of her, proud, black, elegant, beautiful, and bursting with talent and heart in the middle of that place is indelibly imprinted on my mind, and I take heart. This is how we honour those who have come before. We cannot change what has been, but we can shape what is to come, and I feel a powerful drive to do just that. We can reclaim these spaces and work within them. We can cook there, eat there, work there, find joy there.

It is, to my mind, actually imperative that we do. The relationships of the past inform but do not control who we are now, or what we do next. The food that we create is a vessel for liberation and joy. It can be healing, it can bring together the chequered past to create a unified future. YES, I believe that food is powerful in that way.

The family who have been running the house are lovely, but they are handing it over. Our dear friend Ronald, a hotelier who lives in Antigua, is thinking of taking it on. It's a potent place that feels like it's just waiting to be filled with gorgeous food, music, and people. Ronald has some stunning plans to transform it, and the idea of reclaiming a place for new generations where such great pain has been wrought holds huge magnetism for me. I can't help but conjure plans for feasting there. My head is full of yams, eddoes, breadfruit roasting whole in embers, curried conchs, barbecuing chicken, and stewing peas and plantains and fungee and on and on. If Ronald decides to take it on we will do something beautiful together here, I can feel it, but I'll have to wait and see what happens.

Tonight, I need to cook and I need it to be both invigorating and healing. I need in some way for it to reach out to touch what the brilliant academic and author, professor Jessica B. Harris (author of *High on the Hog*), calls the African hand in the kitchen. My brothers, my sisters, our mothers, our fathers, our grands and great grands and great great great grands... we feel you, we are you.

ON THE MENU TODAY

AROMATIC SHRIMP CURRY

GREEN BANANA AND COCONUT
DUMPLINGS

FRESH LEMONADE

AUBERGINE, SPINACH, & OKRA
CHOP-UP

WADADLI KITCHEN ORANGE,
GINGER, & CHILLI AUBERGINE

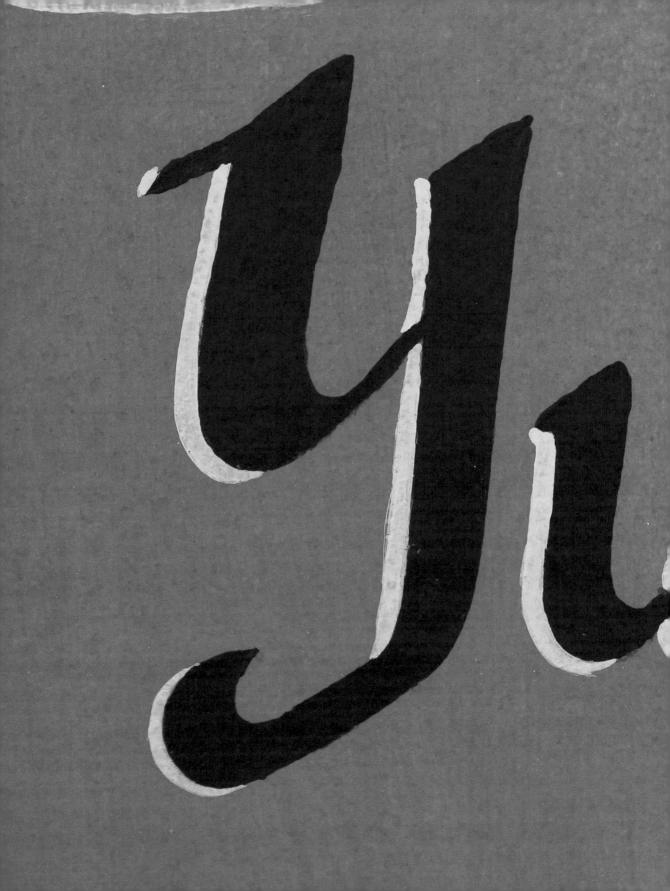

m!

Aromatic shrimp curry

Serves 4
Prep time 10 minutes, plus 20 minutes marinating time
Cook time 40 minutes

This is one of those brilliant I-can't-believe-it-was-so-quick dishes that comes together in under an hour. The fragrant broth is packed with succulent prawns.

450g (1lb) king prawns (jumbo shrimp), peeled and deveined

For the green seasoning marinade

2 jalapeños, or other chillies of your choice, finely chopped

2 tbsp chopped chives

1 tbsp Green Seasoning (see page 110)

pinch each of salt and freshly ground black pepper

For the curry sauce

1 tbsp rapeseed (canola) oil

2 onions, very thinly sliced

2 garlic cloves, grated

1 red chilli, chopped

2 tsp ground cumin

2 tsp ground coriander

2 tsp ground turmeric

2 tbsp Caribbean curry powder

1 tsp ground cinnamon

1 tbsp Tamarind Chutney (see page 119)

1 tomato, finely chopped

1 x 400ml (13.5fl oz) can of coconut milk

chopped coriander (cilantro) and/or fresh chilli, to serve

Put the prawns in a medium bowl and add all the marinade ingredients. Mix well and rub the marinade into the prawns with your hands so that all the prawns are well coated. Refrigerate and leave to marinate for about 20 minutes.

Meanwhile, to make the curry sauce, get a medium, high-sided frying pan over a low–medium heat and pour in the oil. When the oil is hot, add the onions and cook down for 10–15 minutes until soft and fragrant. Add the garlic and chilli and cook for a further 3 minutes.

Add the cumin, coriander, turmeric, curry powder, and cinnamon to the pan and cook, stirring, for 1 minute. Add the tamarind chutney, chopped tomato, coconut milk and 350ml (1½ cups) of water. Bring to a steady simmer for 5 minutes.

Heat a griddle pan or a heavy-based frying pan until red hot, then chuck on the marinated prawns, cooking on each side for around 2 minutes until nicely charred all over. Transfer the prawns to the curry sauce and simmer for around 4 minutes to bring it all together. Finish the curry with a sprinkling of some freshly chopped coriander (cilantro) and/or chillies.

Serve with roti or plain or Coconut Rice (see page 67).

Green banana & coconut dumplings

Makes about 16
Prep time 10 minutes, plus 1 hour 20 minutes soaking and resting
Cook time 7–8 minutes

A boiled dumpling like this is quintessentially Caribbean. It's not pretty, it's not even light, but it sure is gooood!

50g (⅗ cup) desiccated
   (dried shredded) coconut

pinch of white sugar

100ml (generous ⅓ cup) coconut milk

2 large green bananas

300g (2¼ cups) self-raising flour

1½ tsp salt

Soak the desiccated coconut and sugar in the coconut milk for 20 minutes.

Peel and grate the bananas, then combine the grated bananas with the flour, soaked coconut, and ½ teaspoon of the salt in a bowl. Use your hands to mix everything together until you get a dough with a pliable consistency. You may need to add a splash of water or a little more flour to achieve this (depending on how wet your green bananas are). The dough should be soft, but not too sticky. Cover the bowl with cling film (plastic wrap) or a damp kitchen towel and set aside at room temperature for 1 hour.

Fill a large pot almost full with water and set over a high heat. Add the remaining 1 teaspoon of salt, cover the pot with a lid and bring to the boil.

Pinch off a walnut-sized piece of dough and roll it into a ball shape. Use the side of your hand to slightly flatten the top. Repeat to make about 16 dumplings in total.

Drop around a third of the dumplings into the pot of boiling water, taking care not to overcrowd it – you will need to cook these in at least a few separate batches depending on the size of your pot. Cook the first batch for 7–8 minutes with the lid on. Stir the dumplings every couple of minutes so that they don't stick to each other or to the bottom of the pot. They will rise to the top of the water and float as they cook through. Remove from the water with a slotted spoon and drain on kitchen paper (paper towels). Repeat the cooking process until you have cooked all the dumplings before serving.

Fresh lemonade

Serves 6
Prep time 10 minutes
Cook time 5 minutes

At weekends when I was a child, Mum would often make homemade lemonade. It's SO easy, refreshing, and zingy. The perfect jug of delicious on any table.

juice of 12 lemons (about 450ml/ scant 2 cups juice)

100g (½ cup) caster (superfine) sugar (add more if you like it sweeter)

40g (1½oz) fresh ginger, peeled and grated

ice, to serve

sparkling or still water, to serve

Add the lemon juice to a saucepan with the sugar, ginger, and 200ml (scant 1 cup) water. Set over a medium heat and warm through gently, stirring, until the sugar has dissolved.

Leave to cool, then place in the fridge until chilled to your liking. To serve, pour half a glass of the lemonade over ice, and top up with sparkling or still water.

Aubergine, spinach, & okra chop-up

Serves 8 as a side
Prep time 10 minutes
Cook time 30 minutes

Chop-up is actually exactly what it says it is – a silky, slippery mix of chopped up iron-rich vegetables and black-eyed beans. One of those dishes that, for sure, makes a little go a long way. If I'm feeling a bit low-energy or I've been burning the proverbial candle at both ends, a day or two of exercise and chop-up, alongside some grilled fish or roasted roots sets me right back up. Try it!

neutral oil, such as rapeseed (canola) or sunflower oil, for frying

1 large onion, thinly sliced

5 garlic cloves, finely chopped

1 tbsp pimento peppers (baby sweet peppers), finely chopped

12 small–medium firm okra, thinly sliced

300g (10oz) diced courgette (zucchini)

400g (14oz) diced aubergine (eggplant)

1 x 200g (7oz) can of cooked black-eyed beans (black-eyed peas)

250ml (1 cup plus 1 tbsp) vegetable or chicken stock

300g (10oz) fresh spinach leaves

6½ tbsp butter (optional)

salt and freshly ground black pepper

Add the oil to a large pot and set over a medium–low heat. Gently sauté the onion and garlic until golden brown. Add the pimento peppers and fry for a further 5 minutes until softened. Add the okra, courgette, and aubergine, stir gently and cook for around 15 minutes to allow the okra to soften slightly.

Next, add the black-eyed beans, stir gently, then add the stock. Give the pan another little stir, then add the spinach. Put a lid on the pot and let the spinach steam through and wilt. Uncover the pan, season to taste with salt and pepper and stir through the butter to finish (if using).

Serve the chop-up on its own or under lamb or roast chicken or roast vegetables – it's delish!

Wadadli Kitchen orange, ginger, & chilli aubergine

Serves 4
Prep time 15 minutes
Cook time 30 minutes

At Wadadli Kitchen we came up with this while searching for a way that vegans could enjoy the flavours of our chicken wings. These aubergine pieces are crisp on the outside, soft on the inside, and drenched in THAT syrup. The syrup recipe makes more than you will need but leftovers are delicious for grilling, marinating, or glazing anything you like. All the yum...

3 aubergines (eggplants), each cut into 8 large cubes

neutral oil, such as rapeseed (canola) or sunflower oil, for deep-frying

For the coating

200g (1⅓ cups) potato starch

2 tsp garlic powder

2 tsp ground turmeric

salt and freshly ground black pepper, to taste

For the orange, ginger, and chilli syrup

grated zest and juice of 2 oranges

1 Scotch bonnet, bashed

1 long red chilli, bashed

10g (⅓oz) dried chilli flakes

120g (4½oz) fresh ginger, peeled and sliced

3 whole garlic cloves, peeled

400g (2 cups) granulated sugar

2 star anise

2 tsp green cardamom pods

To serve

large handful of chopped coriander (cilantro)

grated zest of ½ orange

To make the syrup, add all the syrup ingredients to a medium saucepan along with 1 litre (4⅓ cups) water and bring to the boil. Reduce until the mixture is thick enough to coat the back of a spoon. Once done, leave to cool and then pass through a sieve. Set aside.

Stir together the coating ingredients in a bowl, then toss the aubergine (eggplant) pieces in the mixture until they are evenly coated all over.

Heat the oil in a deep-fat fryer or heavy-based saucepan to 180°C (350°F). To test whether the oil is hot enough, drop in a cube of white bread. If it bubbles straight away and goes golden, then the oil is ready for frying.

Fry the aubergine pieces in batches until they are crispy. Remove from the oil with a slotted spoon and place on a plate lined with kitchen paper (paper towels) to drain any excess oil. Continue until they are all cooked.

Toss the fried aubergine in half of the orange, ginger, and chilli syrup (keeping the rest in a sealed container in the fridge for other recipes) and serve it up. Finish with a sprinkling of chopped coriander (cilantro) and extra grated orange zest.

Doubles

Makes 6–8
Prep time 30 minutes, plus 2–3 hours resting time
Cook time 10 minutes

I was first introduced to doubles by my dear Trinidadian friend, Lesley Anne Saunders, and it was honestly love at first bite. Puffy bara flatbread with the rich, curry-seasoned chana, zingy cucumber relish, and a final punch of tamarind chutney and glorious hot sauce. It's truly one of the most stunning street food inventions I have ever come across – I just adore them!! Double me up!

For the bara flatbread

150g (1¼ cups) split pea or chickpea (gram) flour

100g (¾ cup) plain (all-purpose) flour, plus a little extra if needed

3 tsp baking powder

1 tsp salt

1 tsp ground cumin

1 tsp curry powder

2 garlic cloves, finely grated

1 tsp freshly cracked black pepper

1 Scotch bonnet or hot chilli of your choice, very finely chopped

100ml (generous ⅓ cup) lukewarm water

250ml (1 cup plus 1 tbsp) neutral oil, such as rapeseed (canola) or sunflower oil, for deep-frying, plus extra for greasing

For the topping

Quick Chana Dhal (see page 69)

Tamarind Chutney (see page 119)

hot sauce of your choice

Cucumber Relish (see page 127)

To make the bara dough, combine the split pea or chickpea flour, plain flour, baking powder, salt, cumin, curry powder, garlic, black pepper, and chilli in a large mixing bowl.

Next, we want to bring the mixture together to form a soft, slightly sticky dough. Add a little splash of lukewarm water at a time, mixing until this sticky, soft texture is achieved. If you are worried the dough is too wet to work with, dust with a little extra flour to bring it back to the perfect consistency.

Splash a little oil into the palm of your hands and rub it all over the dough in the bowl. Cover the bowl with a damp kitchen towel and leave the dough to rest at room temperature for 2–3 hours – 3 hours is preferable if you have time.

When you return to the dough, punch it down gently with your hand, then leave for a further 10–15 minutes to rest.

Now lightly oil your hands again and divide the dough into 6–8 equal portions. Lightly oil a work surface and flatten each portion out into a rough circle with the palm of your hand.

Heat the oil in a high sided heavy-based frying pan or wok to 180°C (350°F). To test whether the oil is hot enough, drop in a cube of white bread. If it bubbles straight away and goes golden, then the oil is ready for frying. Fry each piece of dough for just under a minute – be careful not to overcrowd the pan and fry just 1 or 2 at a time. The bara will puff up and become a gorgeous, light golden brown colour when ready. Remove from the oil with a slotted spoon and place on a plate lined with kitchen paper (paper towels) to drain any excess oil.

When you have a pile of cooked breads, tumble the chana dhal on top and serve topped with tamarind chutney, hot sauce, and a cucumber relish... DIVINE!

Curry crab

Serves 6
Prep time 20 minutes, plus 20 minutes
marinating time
Cook time about 15 minutes

Traditionally, blue crab is used for this curry in Tobago and Jamaica, however any fresh, local, or seasonally available species will suffice. Buy your crab from the fishmonger and ask them to prepare it for you. They will remove all the bits you can't eat.

1kg (2¼lb) or roughly 4 small crabs, halved or quartered

juice of 1 lemon or lime

2 tbsp Green Seasoning (see page 110)

1 tsp salt

1 tsp cracked black pepper

2 tbsp ghee, oil, or butter

2 tsp ground cumin

2 tbsp curry powder

1 small onion or shallot, finely diced

2 spring onions (scallions), finely chopped

1 tsp grated fresh ginger

2 garlic cloves, minced (or more to taste)

1 tsp Scotch bonnet, habanero, or chilli of your choice, very finely chopped

1 small, sweet pepper, diced or grated (traditionally the Trinidadian pimento/ seasoning pepper)

2 tsp fish sauce

½ x 400ml (13.5fl oz) can of good quality unsweetened coconut milk, plus more if needed

1 tbsp chopped coriander (cilantro), to garnish

1 tbsp chopped parsley, to garnish

Place the crab in a large bowl with the lemon or lime juice. Cover with enough water to submerge the crabs, then once lightly bathed in the citrus solution to remove impurities, drain, rinse the crabs and pat them dry.

Place the washed crab in another large bowl. Add the green seasoning and salt and pepper and use your hands to make sure all the crab pieces are evenly coated. If the crabs have large claws, crack them at this stage to allow the seasoning to permeate the meat. Place in the fridge and leave to marinate for around 20 minutes.

Once marinated, set a large saucepan over a medium–low heat and add the ghee, oil, or butter. Add the ground cumin and curry powder, stir to combine and gently release the fragrance, then add the onion or shallot, spring onions (scallions), ginger, garlic, chilli, and sweet pepper. Gently cook out the curry base for about 3–5 minutes. Be careful not to burn the spices and add a splash of water if needed.

Add the marinated crab and fish sauce to the pan and stir well to coat in the curry paste. Increase the heat to medium–high and add the coconut milk. Cover and bring to the boil. Once boiling, turn the heat down to a simmer and leave to cook for 8–10 minutes. Add more coconut milk or a splash of water if the sauce dries out too much.

Garnish with coriander (cilantro) and parsley and serve.

Cauliflower & potato curry

Serves 4–6
Prep time 15 minutes
Cook time 40 minutes

1 head of cauliflower (about 550g/1¼lb), broken into small florets

1 tsp Caribbean curry powder

2 garlic cloves

1 cinnamon stick

1 chilli of your choice

2 star anise

2 black cardamom pods

pinch of salt

3–4 waxy potatoes (about 650g/1lb 7oz), sliced

300ml (1¼ cups) rapeseed (canola) oil

200ml (scant 1 cup) coconut milk

2 tbsp Green Seasoning (see page 110)

1½ tbsp unsalted butter

handful of chopped chives, to serve

handful of chopped spring onions (scallions), to serve

For the escovitch pickle

1 white onion

½ yellow pepper, deseeded

½ red pepper, deseeded

½ green pepper, deseeded

250ml (1 cup plus 1 tbsp) white vinegar

1 tbsp plus 2 tsp caster (superfine) sugar

1 tsp allspice berries

1 tsp black peppercorns

1 Scotch bonnet

This is a great midweek meal and a delicious way to bring something new to the humble potato and cauliflower – two ingredients I love but sometimes get a bit bored by. Topping it off with the powerful BAM of escovitch pickle hits just the right uplifting notes to ring the changes.

Start by making the escovitch pickle that will accompany the curry. Slice the onion and peppers evenly and very thinly – I use a mandolin to make it quicker, but a good, sharp knife will do just as well.

Add the vinegar, 3½ tablespoons water, the sugar, spices, and Scotch bonnet to a saucepan. Place over a low heat and stir to dissolve the sugar. This should just take a couple of minutes. Remove from the heat and allow to cool. Once cooled, add the peppers and onions and leave to pickle while you make the curry.

For the curry, parboil the cauliflower florets in a deep pot of vigorously boiling water, along with the curry powder, garlic, cinnamon stick, chilli, star anise, and cardamom and salt for 5–6 minutes until just beginning to become tender. Remove immediately with a slotted spoon, transfer to a colander to drain and put to one side.

Now, use the same water and parboil the sliced potatoes for around the same time until they are also just becoming tender. Again, remove with a slotted spoon and set aside to drain. Reserve the cooking liquid for later.

Heat 100ml (generous ⅓ cup) of the oil in a heavy-based saucepan or wok over a medium heat. Once the oil is reasonably hot, slip the cauliflower florets into the pan and sauté until they have a deep golden colour. Remove with a slotted spoon and transfer to some kitchen paper (paper towels) to drain. Now, carefully add the rest of the oil and heat again. This time, slip the potatoes in and fry until they take on a lovely golden colour as well – you may need to do this in 2 batches so that the pan is not overcrowded. Remove with a slotted spoon and drain on kitchen paper. Set the pan with the hot oil to one side off the heat to be used again or discarded when cold.

Set another saucepan or wok over a medium heat. Add the cauliflower and potatoes and combine the two ingredients gently. Ladle in about 200ml (scant 1 cup) of the reserved cooking liquid, then add the coconut milk and green seasoning. Simmer gently for about 5–6 minutes. Throw in the butter and let it melt into the curry.

Transfer the curry to a serving dish and top with the escovitch pickle, the chopped chives, and spring onions (scallions) to serve.

Curry-spiced roast parsnips in butter broth

Serves 4 as a side
Prep time 15 minutes
Cook time 45 minutes

This recipe is one of those happy-pottering-around-the-kitchen inventions that you don't know you're even doing until it's done! A gorgeous way of cooking parsnips, all brought together in a golden, silky, buttery broth.

430g (15oz) parsnips (roughly 2 large parsnips), peeled and cut into large chunks

1 cinnamon stick

2 star anise

1 tsp cumin seeds

¼ tsp paprika, plus extra to serve

¼ tsp ground turmeric

1 large chilli, halved lengthways

3½ tbsp rapeseed (canola) oil

3 tbsp cold unsalted butter

Preheat the oven to 200°C fan (220°C/425°F/Gas 7).

Tip all the ingredients, apart from the oil and butter, into a large pot and cover with water. Boil vigorously for around 6 minutes – this should be just enough time for the parsnips to start to become tender. Remove the parsnip pieces from the poaching liquid with a slotted spoon and lay on a piece of kitchen paper (paper towel) for a few minutes to dry off. Reserve the poaching liquid.

Slip a roasting tray with the oil into the preheated oven for about 10 minutes. When the oil is nice and hot, remove from the oven and carefully lay the parboiled parsnips into the tray. Mix to coat them with the oil, then return to the oven and roast for around 35 minutes until golden, shaking and turning the parsnips every now and again.

Meanwhile, strain the poaching liquid into a bowl, then tip it back into the pot and bring to a rolling boil for around 15 minutes, or until reduced by half (you should be left with around 100ml (generous ⅓ cup). Whisk in the cold butter until melted and combined.

Transfer the parsnips from the roasting tray to a warmed serving dish, then pour the butter broth over the top. Dust with a little paprika and serve hot.

Chocolate curry goat

Serves 4–6
Prep time 20 minutes
Cook time 3–4 hours

neutral oil, such as rapeseed (canola) or sunflower oil, for frying

300g (10½oz) onion, blitzed in a food processor

70g (2½oz) garlic cloves, blitzed in a food processor

10g (⅓oz) black cardamom pods

10g (⅓oz) green cardamom pods

10g (⅓oz) star anise

3 cinnamon sticks

1 tbsp whole cloves

20g (¾oz) ground cumin

20g (¾oz) ground coriander

2 Scotch bonnet chillies, finely chopped

100ml (½ cup) molasses, or use treacle or carob molasses

1kg (2¼lb) chopped goat or mutton, preferably on the bone

2 sprigs of thyme

2 fresh bay leaves

2 litres (8½ cups) lamb or beef stock

splash of red wine

2 large tomatoes, finely chopped

80g (2¾oz) 70% dark (bittersweet) chocolate

1½ tbsp butter

salt and freshly ground black pepper

To garnish

handful of chopped coriander (cilantro)

handful of chopped spring onions (scallions)

handful of flat-leaf parsley

This might well be the recipe I've been preoccupied with the longest in my life – and that really is saying something. Curry goat is an iconic Caribbean dish, of course, and everyone has their own take on it. After years of feeding the family and getting their verdict on it, this is the Oliver/Cherry family all-time favourite version! You can serve it with rice and peas, white rice, with or in a roti. At the Wadadli Kitchen we tumble it over crisp fries and it goes down a storm.

And yes, it's got chocolate in it! I took the inspiration from a Mexican mole, and found that the rich dark bitterness of 70% and above chocolate was the perfect way to finish my curry goat. Don't be scared, gwaaaan, give it a go!

Add a splash of oil to a large, heavy-based saucepan or casserole dish and set over a low–medium heat. Chuck in the blitzed onions and garlic and let them sweat for a few minutes until slightly softened. Add the whole spices and fry for 5 minutes. Pour a little more oil into the pan, then add the ground spices and fry for a further 5 minutes.

Add the Scotch bonnets, molasses, meat, thyme sprigs, bay leaves, and a little more oil again. Turn up the heat and cook for 15–20 minutes until the meat is brown and caramelized, stirring intermittently.

Add the stock, red wine, and tomatoes to the pan so that the liquid just covers the meat. Turn the heat back down to low and cook for 2–3 hours until the meat is tender, adding a little more stock if the liquid level starts to get too low. After the first 1½ hours of cooking time, check the seasoning and add some salt and pepper to taste.

When the meat is tender, check the seasoning again and adjust if needed. Add the chocolate and let it melt into the curry. Simmer gently for a final 20 minutes, then add the butter and stir through before serving.

Serve garnished with a handful of chopped coriander (cilantro), spring onions (scallions), and flat-leaf parsley.

Wadadli Kitchen curry mushrooms

Serves 4
Prep time 15 minutes
Cook time 35 minutes

150g (5½oz) oyster mushrooms, torn in half

250g (9oz) chestnut mushrooms or white button mushrooms, cut into quarters

40g (1½oz) dried porcini mushrooms

400ml (1¾ cups) boiling water

1 tsp yeast extract, such as Marmite

2 tbsp rapeseed (canola) oil

20g (¾oz) fresh ginger, peeled and finely grated

30g (1oz) garlic, finely grated

1–2 Scotch bonnet chillies to taste, seeds removed and finely chopped

1 small onion, thinly sliced

2 bay leaves

2 tsp cornflour (corn starch)

6 spring onions (scallions), thinly sliced

small handful of coriander (cilantro), finely chopped

salt and freshly ground black pepper

For the marinade

60g (2oz) minced garlic

4½ tbsp rapeseed (canola) oil

1 tsp flaky sea salt

1 tsp freshly ground black pepper

1 tsp ground turmeric

2 tsp ground cumin

1 heaped tsp ground coriander

1 heaped tsp ground allspice

1 tsp chopped thyme leaves

1 tsp chopped oregano

1 tsp miso paste

This recipe is the result of several different brains at our Wadadli restaurant project. We wanted to come up with a plant-based dish to load onto fries and we finally hit on this. Rich, dark, and velvety... it works a treat!

Preheat the oven to 200°C fan (220°C/425°F/Gas 7).

Mix all the marinade ingredients together in a small bowl.

Remember to clean all the mushrooms if you haven't already. In a separate large bowl, mix the oyster and chestnut or button mushrooms with half of the marinade. Spread the mushrooms out on a baking tray and roast in the preheated oven for 20–25 minutes, or until they are well browned and slightly crispy.

Meanwhile, add the porcini mushrooms to a saucepan with the boiling water. Cover and leave to simmer over a medium heat for 10 minutes.

Remove the porcini mushrooms from the pan. Return the saucepan with the mushroom cooking liquid to a medium heat and add the yeast extract. Leave to simmer, uncovered, for 10–15 minutes until reduced by about half. Roughly chop the porcini mushrooms and set aside.

Add the oil, ginger, garlic, Scotch bonnets, onion, and bay leaves to a large sauté pan over a medium heat. Gently sweat the ingredients down for 10 minutes. Add the remaining marinade and sauté for a further 5 minutes.

Add the roasted mushrooms, chopped porcini mushrooms and reduced mushroom stock and bring to a gentle simmer. Mix the cornflour (corn starch) with a splash of water in a mug to make a slurry and add to the pan, stirring until combined; the sauce should quickly thicken. Season with salt and pepper and turn off the heat.

Top with the spring onions (scallions) and coriander (cilantro) and serve.

Curry shrimp

Serves 4
Prep time 15 minutes, plus 20 minutes marinating time
Cook time 20 minutes

Fragrant and punchy, with juicy prawns and silky coconut milk, curry shrimp sits beautifully in the middle of a family feast. Serve with rice, roti, or dumpling to soak up the really rather excellent curry sauce.

700g (1lb 9oz) fresh or frozen king prawns (jumbo shrimp), peeled and deveined

1 tsp salt

1 tsp fresh cracked black pepper

2 tbsp Green Seasoning (see page 110)

2 tsp ground cumin

2 tbsp curry powder

2 tsp garam masala

4 tbsp coconut oil or cooking oil of your choice

6 curry leaves

1 large onion, finely diced

2 spring onions (scallions), finely chopped

½ red sweet pepper, diced or grated

½ green sweet pepper, diced or grated

2 tomatoes, finely diced

2 garlic cloves, minced

1 small Scotch bonnet, minced (remove the seeds for less spice)

2 sprigs of thyme

1 bay leaf

4 tbsp water or stock of your choice

½ x 400ml (13.5fl oz) can of good quality unsweetened coconut milk

juice of 1 lemon or lime

3 tbsp chopped coriander (cilantro)

Start by placing the shrimp in a big bowl along with the salt, pepper, 1 tablespoon of the green seasoning, 1 teaspoon of the cumin, 1 tablespoon of the curry powder, and 1 teaspoon of the garam masala. Cover and leave to marinate in the fridge for 20 minutes.

Once marinated, set a Dutch pot or a heavy-based saucepan over a medium heat and add half of the oil. Add the curry leaves and stir-fry until the oil becomes fragrant, then add the remaining green seasoning, cumin, curry powder, and garam masala. Tip in the diced onion, spring onions (scallions), peppers, tomatoes, garlic, and Scotch bonnet. Add the thyme and bay leaf and stir in the water or stock. Add the coconut milk and increase the heat to bring the pan to a low boil. Cook for about 15–20 minutes to form a thick curry sauce.

Add the remaining oil to a separate frying pan over a medium–high heat. Sear the shrimp for 2 minutes on each side until they take on some colour, then add them to the curry sauce along with the lemon or lime juice and stir through. Sprinkle over the coriander (cilantro) and serve.

Goat water

Serves 6–8
Prep time 20 minutes
Cook time 2½–3 hours

There are so many versions of stews and curries using goat all over the Caribbean. In Antigua, Saint Kitts, Nevis, and Montserrat it's usually called goat water. The flavour profile of goat water often leans more towards cloves and nutmeg, but you'll also find the usual suspects such as allspice, Scotch bonnets, and a herb that is much beloved in Caribbean cookery: thyme. Goat water tends to be a touch lighter than curry goat, with the merest wisp of sweet aroma in the background.

2kg (4½lb) bone-in goat or mutton, diced

2 tbsp neutral oil, such as rapeseed (canola) or sunflower oil, or lard

1 tbsp jaggery or dark soft brown sugar

4 sprigs of thyme or marjoram

1 tsp ground mace

2 tsp ground allspice

2 tsp ground cloves

1 litre (4⅓ cups) chicken, beef, or lamb stock

4 tbsp Green Seasoning (see page 110)

1 tsp Caribbean browning sauce

2 bay leaves

2 dried chillies (such as pasilla, guajillo, ancho, etc.)

1–2 Scotch bonnet(s) or chilli(es) of your choice, diced (keep in mind that your green seasoning already contains chilli)

1 tbsp molasses

1–2 tbsp dark rum (preferably Antiguan)

salt and freshly ground black pepper

finely chopped spring onion (scallion) and fresh herbs or chillies, to garnish

In a large mixing bowl or container, wash the meat in a solution made with water and a splash of lemon juice or white vinegar. This step is entirely optional, but it is considered key in Caribbean culture. Pat dry with kitchen paper (paper towels) and set aside.

Meanwhile, set a large saucepan over a medium–low heat and add the oil or lard. Add the jaggery or brown sugar and allow it to gently melt and caramelize for a couple of minutes, being careful not to burn it. Add the goat or mutton and cook until coated in caramelized sugar and browned all over. Add the thyme or marjoram, mace, allspice, and cloves. Pour in the stock and bring to the boil.

Once boiling, add the green seasoning, browning sauce, bay leaves, dried chillies, fresh chilli, molasses, and salt and pepper to taste. Reduce the heat, cover the pan and let the goat water simmer for 2–3 hours, or until the meat is lovely and tender.

Garnish with finely chopped spring onions (scallions) and fresh herbs of your choice, or finely chopped chillies. Serve immediately alongside bread and/or dumplings.

Curry chicken

Serves 6-8
Prep time 30 minutes, plus marinating time
Cook time 1 hour 10 minutes

Simple, delicious, and a proper family staple, curry chicken is familiar and comforting. I LOVE a second-day pot of curry, and this recipe is no exception – if you make a big enough pot it will see you through a couple of dinners in the middle of the week. This is also one of those many moments you'll be glad you took my advice to keep a big jar of green seasoning in the fridge.

8 chicken thighs and/or legs, skin on and bone in

3 tbsp Green Seasoning (see page 110)

1 tsp salt

3 garlic cloves, finely grated

1 Scotch bonnet or a chilli of your choice, finely chopped

2 tbsp ghee or rapeseed (canola) oil

1 large onion, diced

3 tbsp Caribbean curry powder

375ml (generous 1½ cups) chicken stock

2 tbsp chopped coriander (cilantro), to garnish

Wash the chicken in a solution made with water and a splash of lemon juice or white vinegar. This step is entirely optional, but it is considered key in Caribbean culture. Pat the meat dry with kitchen paper (paper towels).

Place the chicken in a large bowl and add the green seasoning, salt, and roughly half of the garlic and chilli. Mix with your hands so that the chicken is well coated. Set the chicken aside in the fridge to marinate, ideally overnight or for a minimum of 30 minutes.

When you are ready to cook, set a large saucepan over a medium–high heat and add the ghee or oil. Sear the marinated chicken pieces until nicely browned on all sides, then remove them from the pan to a plate and set aside.

Lower the heat to medium–low, then add the onion and remaining garlic and chilli. Lightly sauté for 5 minutes until slightly softened. Add the curry powder and just a little splash of water – enough to form a paste. Gently cook this out for 2 minutes, being careful not to burn the spices.

Add the browned chicken back into the pan and stir well, making sure it is completely coated in the curry paste. Increase the heat to medium–high, add the stock, cover the pan and simmer for about 1 hour until the chicken is cooked through and tender.

Serve immediately, garnished with chopped coriander (cilantro), alongside the rice or bread of your choice.

Sauces, sides, marinades, & seasoning

Thinking about green seasoning leads me to a whole train of thought on seasonings, marinades, and sauces, whether it's on the side or at the heart of a dish. The word seasoning means something very different in Caribbean cooking than it does in a Eurocentric kitchen vocabulary. In Europe, when we refer to something as seasoned, we generally mean the salt and pepper, but when we talk about seasoning in a Caribbean kitchen, it means a whole lot more! It's where the magic happens – chillies, little seasoning peppers, a whole world of herbs and bush, garlic, ginger, oils, and potions. There is a common misconception that Caribbean food is just hot – like chilli hot – but that is truthfully not the case. We seek flavour and depth, not just heat in our food. It's actually more about fragrance than heat.

Friday 29th January

Vicky the car park meat dealer

Slow-cooked cuts of meat just feel like home to me, whether lamb, pork belly, chicken or brisket... it's all the yum. I lived in Cyprus as a child and that soft, yielding, caramelized slow-roast lamb vibe just sweeps me up and holds me in its loving arms. I adore it.

Good quality meat can be very expensive to buy in Antigua – often in supermarkets it's not the best quality, as it's imported and filled with all kinds of crappy chemicals. I had a tip off, though, about a natural farmer here in Antigua at a place called Hall Valley Farm, who is producing truly great quality meat and not charging crazy prices for it. I got the number, put in my order and then went to meet Vicky and Adrian yesterday in a car park (parking lot) in Falmouth to pick up my incredible meat. All very exciting and clandestine. The produce is SO good, I got a whole shoulder of lamb, a pork belly and some chicken wings and thighs for my freezer.

Green seasoning is a ubiquitous mix that you'll find all over the Caribbean. It will slightly differ from house to house and island to island, but it is powerfully herbal, packs a punch and all Caribbean heritage cooks I know use it ALL the time. It features in so many recipes in this book and is such a brilliant shortcut to getting those layers of flavour into your food without having to do loads of prep every time you've got to cook. So, make a BIG batch and get it in your fridge – you'll be glad that you did. If you're anything like me, you'll need to make it once a week.

ON THE MENU TODAY

GREEN SEASONING & RUM PORCHETTA WITH RUM-DIPPED CRACKLING

SWEET POTATO & CARAMELIZED ONION STUFFED ROTIS

CHARRED BLACK PINEAPPLE CHOW

Green seasoning

Makes about 500ml (generous 2 cups)
Prep time 15 minutes

2 sprigs of thyme

10g (⅓oz) fresh bay leaves

1 small bunch of flat-leaf parsley

1 small bunch of coriander (cilantro)

4 spring onions (scallions)

10 garlic cloves, peeled

1 green chilli or 1 Scotch bonnet, depending
on how much heat you like

6 little Caribbean seasoning peppers (about
20g/¾oz), or a mix of red, yellow, and/or
green mini sweet peppers

½ white onion

400ml (1¾ cups) cold pressed rapeseed
(canola) oil or any neutral oil

salt and freshly ground black pepper

food processor

airtight jar

Green seasoning! What a genius thing it is. Green seasoning makes your entire life so much easier. A glorious concoction of herbs and a little heat and garlic, which turns the most pedestrian pot or piece of protein into the best version of itself. In this book, green seasoning comes up a LOT, so make a batch, get it in a jar and whack it in the fridge. If you use it as much as I do, you'll make it at least once a week – it's SO worth it. Green seasoning is found all over the Caribbean and is more than just a short-cut to flavour, it's the heart and soul of Caribbean seasoning. In European cooking, there's celery, garlic, onions, maybe a little carrot, as the starting point for so many one-pot dishes. Proteins are seasoned with salt and pepper. In the Caribbean, we have all that PLUS green seasoning to kick things off.

Add all the ingredients to a food processor and season to taste with salt and pepper. Whizz to the consistency of a salsa verde and keep in an airtight jar in the fridge for up to 2–3 weeks.

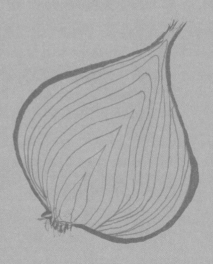

Green feta dip

100g (3½oz) feta, crumbled

3 tbsp full-fat crème fraîche or natural plain yogurt

1–2 tbsp Green Seasoning (see page 110)

2 tsp runny honey

grated zest and juice of 1 lemon

big pinch of salt

Add all the ingredients to a small bowl. Mix gently to combine, then check and adjust the seasoning to your taste. It will keep in the fridge for 2–3 days.

Green seasoning salsa verde

2 tsp finely chopped capers

grated zest and juice of 1 lemon

3 tbsp Green Seasoning (see page 110)

¼ bunch flat-leaf parsley, leaves picked and finely chopped

4 canned anchovies, drained and finely chopped

splash of extra virgin cold pressed rapeseed (canola) oil

1 green chilli, finely chopped

Add all the ingredients to a small bowl and mix until combined. Taste the salsa and add a little salt if you think it needs it (the anchovies are already quite salty, so check and check again before adding). It will keep in the fridge for up to 1 week.

Green seasoning butter

250g (2 sticks) unsalted butter, softened

80ml (⅓ cup) extra virgin cold pressed rapeseed (canola) oil

2 tbsp Green Seasoning (see page 110)

Beat all the ingredients together in a food processor, then transfer to a bowl or ramekins and refrigerate until needed. Use on top of fried fish, grilled steak, grilled lamb chops, or barbecued chicken thighs – anything you can melt it on to add flavour! It will keep for up to 1 week.

Green seasoning & rum porchetta with rum-dipped crackling

Serves 6–8
Prep time 2 days
Cook time 3½ hours

I once made a TV show in Glasgow and met a lovely Glaswegian-Italian family. The mother, Gilda, taught me how she makes her porchetta, and I fell in love with it. So, when I got home, I started playing around with Caribbean flavours in place of the Italian ones, and this is what I came up with using her technique... it's pretty lush!

2.8kg (6¼lb) boned and skinned pork belly (skin to be used for crackling)

3 tbsp sea salt

4 tbsp Green Seasoning (see page 110)

7 tbsp dark or golden rum

splash of rapeseed (canola) oil

freshly ground black pepper

For the rum-soaked crackling

380g (13oz) pork skin

150ml (⅔ cup) dark or golden rum

3 tbsp sea salt

100g (½ cup) sugar

For the gravy

3 shallots, finely chopped

5 tbsp coconut vinegar (or other vinegar of your choice)

300ml (1¼ cups) chicken stock

cooking juices from the tray

roll of thin cooking string/twine

Day 1 Lay the pork belly in a large plastic lidded tub, flesh-side down. Take 1½ tablespoons of the sea salt and evenly rub it into the meat. Do the same with 2 tablespoons of the green seasoning, then pour over 3 tablespoons of the rum. Cover with a lid and leave in the fridge for 24 hours.

Day 2 Repeat this process the next day, this time adding 1 tablespoon of the salt, the remaining 2 tablespoons of the green seasoning, and 2 tablespoons of the remaining rum. Cover with a lid and leave in the fridge again for 24 hours.

Day 3 Remove the pork from the fridge about 20–30 minutes before you want to cook and leave it to come up to room temperature.

Preheat the oven to 120°C fan (140°C/285°F/Gas 1).

Remove the pork belly from its container and lay on a wide cutting board. Starting with the narrow end, roll the belly tightly in on itself like a Swiss roll. Hold the rolled belly in one hand and tightly wrap some cooking string/twine around the whole length of the joint before tying up the loose ends tightly to secure. Place the joint in a large roasting tray.

Take the last ½ tablespoon of salt and sprinkle it over the pork. Grind some black pepper liberally along the joint. Sprinkle with 1 tablespoon of the rum, then drizzle the oil down the length of the joint. Cover the whole thing with tin foil and slip into the preheated oven.

After 2 hours, take the foil off, pour the cooking juices into a bowl and set aside. Splash the last 1 tablespoon of rum in the bottom of the roasting tray and return, uncovered, to the oven for a further 25–30 minutes.

Turn the oven temperature up to 180°C fan (200°C/400°F/ Gas 6) and cook for another 35 minutes until the pork is golden brown all over and cooked through. Rest the pork for at least 30 minutes once cooked.

Whilst the pork is resting, make the crackling. Lay the pork skin on a board and drizzle 2 tablespoons of the rum onto the flesh side. Turn the pork skin-side up, and rub the sea salt into both sides. Take two flat baking sheets and lay a sheet of baking parchment on one. Add the pork skin to the lined baking sheet, then place another sheet of baking parchment on top and cover with the other baking tray. Slip into the hot oven at 200°C fan (220°C/425°F/Gas 7) for around 45–60 minutes and roast until crisp and brittle.

Melt the sugar and the remaining rum together over a low heat in a saucepan, then brush over the cooked crisp crackling. Break up the crackling and leave to one side.

To make the gravy, place a medium saucepan over a medium heat and add the shallots and vinegar. Let it reduce for about 6–7 minutes, then add the chicken stock and reserved pork roasting juices. Reduce for a further 5–10 minutes until thickened and bubbling.

Carve the porchetta into thin slices, then ladle over the gravy and serve with a bit of the rum-soaked crackling on the side.

Sweet potato & caramelized onion stuffed rotis

Serves 8
Prep time 2 hours 20 minutes
Cook time 20 minutes

I love a stuffed bread of ANY kind, and this version is glorious! Easy and fabulous!

For the dough

400g (3¼ cups) plain (all-purpose) flour, plus extra for dusting

2 pinches of salt

200ml (scant 1 cup) warm water

3½ tbsp olive oil

neutral oil, such as rapeseed (canola) or sunflower oil, for frying

For the stuffing

1 large sweet potato (about 300g/10oz, preferably white sweet potato), peeled and cut into bite-sized chunks

1 tbsp unsalted butter

1 tbsp olive oil

1 onion, grated

4 garlic cloves, grated

salt and freshly ground black pepper

To make the dough, combine the flour and salt in a large bowl. Gradually mix in the warm water and the olive oil, adding a little of both at the same time or alternately, until a dough forms. Tip the dough out onto a lightly floured work surface and knead for at least 10 minutes until smooth. Return the dough to the bowl and cover with a damp kitchen towel. Leave to rest for 2 hours at room temperature.

Meanwhile, for the stuffing, boil the sweet potato in a large pan of water with a pinch of salt. When the potato is soft, drain it and mash it up. Season with salt and pepper. Set aside.

Add the butter and oil to a small frying pan over a medium heat. When the butter has melted, chuck in the grated onion and garlic and cook for 10–15 minutes stirring occasionally, until caramelized and deliciously sweet.

Combine the mashed sweet potato with the caramelized onions and roll the mixture into 8 little equally sized balls. Set aside.

Divide the rested dough into 8 equal pieces. Roll out a piece of dough on a lightly floured work surface to a 10cm (4in) circle. Take one of the sweet potato stuffing balls and place in the middle of the dough circle. Bring the edges up around the stuffing and seal by pinching the ends together. With the sealed side face-down on the work surface, gently roll out again, using just light pressure, to around 15cm (6in). Some of the stuffing may slightly pop out, but it's not a disaster, just gently carry on until the roti is flat. Repeat this process for the rest until you have 8 stuffed rotis.

Add a splash of neutral oil to a flat, heavy, iron frying pan or a non-stick pan over a medium–low heat. Fry each stuffed roti until golden on both sides. Remove from the pan and serve.

Charred black pineapple chow

Serves 4 as a side
Prep time 15 minutes
Cook time 10 minutes

A chow is a simple yet effective, hot and slightly sweet salsa, really. This one is made with the Antiguan black pineapple, which is a particularly tender and flavoursome component. If you can't find black pineapple, use anything you can get your hands on instead – regular pineapple, apple, or mango all work well.

neutral oil, such as rapeseed (canola) or sunflower oil, for frying

1 black pineapple (or see above), peeled, cored and diced into 2cm (¾in) pieces

2 tbsp Green Seasoning (see page 110)

3 jalapeños or chillies of your choice, finely chopped

4 spring onions (scallions) finely chopped

½ handful of flat-leaf parsley

a couple of sprigs of coriander (cilantro), leaves only

juice of 1 lime

salt and freshly ground black pepper

Heat a heavy-based, non-stick frying pan over a high heat. Add a tiny splash of oil and sauté the diced pineapple until it takes on a good, dark colour. You can push this as far as you like, even until some parts are just turning black; about 10 minutes. Remove the pineapple from the pan to a bowl and leave to cool.

Once cool, add the green seasoning, jalapeños or chillies, spring onions (scallions), herbs, and lime juice to the pineapple in the bowl and mix well. Taste to check the seasoning, adding salt and pepper if needed. Excellent served with Corn Fritters (see page 121).

Wadadli Kitchen roast chilli hot sauce

Makes 1.2 litres (5 cups)
Prep time 10 minutes
Cook time 40 minutes

**The hot sauce to end all hot sauce –
this makes your lips tingle and kicks my
plate into the stratosphere. Roasting
the ingredients brings out their natural
sweetness, so it's hot, smoky, AND it's
full of flavour, not just heat.**

10 Scotch bonnets if you like it really hot,
   or use 6 for a milder version

4 large onions

2 fat garlic bulbs

50g (1¾oz) thyme, leaves picked
   and chopped

25g (scant 1oz) ground allspice

250g (9oz) cherry tomatoes

splash of neutral oil, such as rapeseed
   (canola) or sunflower oil

250ml (1 cup plus 1 tbsp) white vinegar

125g (⅔ cup) dark soft brown sugar

salt and freshly ground black pepper

food processor
airtight bottle or jar

Preheat the oven to 180°C fan (200°C/400°F/Gas 6).

Destalk the Scotch bonnets, slice them open and remove
the seeds if you don't like it extra hot! Peel the onions and
cut each one into roughly 8 pieces. Peel the garlic cloves.

Add the Scotch bonnets, onions, and garlic to a roasting tray
with the thyme, allspice, 200g (7oz) of the cherry tomatoes,
and oil. Season with salt and pepper. Give the ingredients a
good toss, then stick them in the preheated oven to roast for
40 minutes, or until everything is soft and slightly charred.
Remove from the oven and allow to cool.

Add the cooled roasted veg to a food processor with the
remaining cherry tomatoes and the vinegar and sugar. Blend
until super smooth, then check and adjust the seasoning to
your taste.

Decant the chilli sauce into a bottle or jar, cover
with a lid and keep in the fridge for up to 2–3 weeks.

Tamarind chutney

Makes 60ml (¼ cup)
Prep time 2 minutes
Cook time 5–7 minutes

I so love the unique sour nature of tamarind. It's almost like a connector between sweet, salty, and savoury – somehow it seems to sing to all of those sensations. A spoonful of tamarind chutney will bring any dish to life.

4 tbsp tamarind paste

2 tbsp sugar (demerara or dark soft brown sugar work best)

2 tsp coriander seeds

2 tsp ground allspice

2 tbsp Green Seasoning (see page 110)

airtight jar or container

Put all the ingredients into a small saucepan with 80ml (scant ⅓ cup) of water. Set over a medium–low heat and warm through, stirring now and again, until everything is melted and combined.

Leave to cool, then transfer to a sealed jar or container and store in the fridge to use as needed. The chutney should keep well for 3–4 weeks.

Aunty Linnette's corn fritters

Makes about 15
Prep time 15 minutes
Cook time 4 minutes

My darling mother-in-law, Linnette Smith, was one of kindest, smartest, and most glamorous women I've ever known. When I first got together with Garfield, she welcomed me into the family with open arms and made me feel immediately at home – for this I will always be grateful to her. I think of her often and we all miss her a lot.

Linnette was one of the best cooks, too. This is her fritter recipe, which I use as the basis for any fritter batter I make. We serve these in honour of her on our Wadadli Kitchen menu. We love a fritter in the Caribbean... put it this way, if something's not nailed down, we'll probably at some point try to fritter it! Here's to you, dear Linnette.

100g (3½oz) drained canned sweetcorn

2 spring onions (scallions), finely chopped

20g (¾oz) mixed finely chopped red and green peppers

2 eggs

1 tbsp sparkling water

40g (generous ¼ cup) plain (all-purpose) flour

½ tsp baking powder

large pinch of cayenne pepper

large pinch of paprika

large pinch of ground allspice

pinch each of salt and freshly ground black pepper

300–400ml (1¼–1¾ cups) neutral oil, such as rapeseed (canola) or sunflower oil, for frying

Combine all the ingredients, apart from the oil, together in a big mixing bowl and give them a good, proper stir until thoroughly mixed. The mixture should be a spoonable consistency – if it seems too wet, add a little more flour.

Heat the oil in a deep-fat fryer or heavy-based saucepan or frying pan. To test whether the oil is hot enough, drop in a cube of white bread. If it bubbles straight away and goes golden, then the oil is ready for frying.

Take a dessert spoon and gently lower spoonfuls of the mixture into the hot oil – be careful, don't drop the mixture in, lower it gently! You may need a second spoon to push the mixture off the first spoon. Depending on the size of your pan, you may need to cook the fritters in a few batches to avoid overcrowding the pan.

The fritters should take around 4 minutes to cook. Use a long-handled metal, slotted spoon to turn them a little in the oil. When they are golden all over, remove the fritters from the pan and transfer to a plate lined with some kitchen paper (paper towels) to drain the excess oil.

Serve with a zingy dip such as Charred Black Pineapple Chow (see page 117).

Luscious mac & cheese

Serves 4–6
Prep time 15 minutes
Cook time 30 minutes

What can I say? It's mac and cheese turned all the way up to 11! Gooey, rich, garlicky goodness.

500g (1lb 2oz) dried macaroni pasta

300g (10oz) Comté

250g (9oz) Gruyère

350g (12oz) strong Cheddar

1 x 410ml (14fl oz) can of evaporated milk

300ml (1¼ cups) full-fat milk

300ml (1⅓ cups) double (heavy) cream

150g (⅔ cup) unsalted butter

100g (¾ cup) plain (all-purpose) flour

1 big tsp hot English mustard or mustard of your choice

For the crumb topping

2 tbsp unsalted butter

4 tbsp rapeseed (canola) oil

6 garlic cloves, grated

100g (3½oz) fine white breadcrumbs (or use panko breadcrumbs if you prefer a crispier finish)

Preheat the oven to 190°C fan (210°C/410°F/Gas 6).

Cook the macaroni in a deep pan of vigorously boiling salted water until tender but still with a little bite left to it; it'll take around 10 minutes. Drain immediately and leave to one side. Whilst this is happening, grate all the cheeses, mix them all together and set aside.

Combine both the milks and the cream together in a jug or cup and keep to one side of the hob (stove). Gently melt the butter in a deep saucepan over a low heat. Add the flour and beat it into the butter with a wooden spoon. When the flour and butter are fully combined, keep stirring for around 4 minutes, then gradually add the milk and cream mixture, bit by bit, beating it in each time to keep the sauce smooth. Next, beat in just over half of the cheese mixture and the mustard. Set aside off the heat.

For the topping, melt the butter and oil together in a wide frying pan. Add the garlic and very gently soften over a low heat for around 4 minutes. Add the breadcrumbs and stir them through the oil. Toast for few minutes, then remove from the heat.

Combine the cooked macaroni with the cheese sauce in an ovenproof dish. Top with the remaining grated cheese and toasted breadcrumbs. Bake in the preheated oven for 15 minutes, until lovely and golden on top. Serve.

Lemon & garlic dressed callaloo

Serves 4 as a side
Prep time 15 minutes
Cook time 5 minutes

Ooh, callaloo!! Leafy, iron-y, glorious goodness. Callaloo actually is a specific leaf, but it's often used as a catch-all term for spinach-y, kale-y, fabulous greens! I adore callaloo, especially this citrusy dressed version. Take this recipe as a starting point and try dressing it with all your favourite things.

splash of rapeseed (canola) oil

½ large bunch of rainbow chard, stalks chopped and leaves roughly shredded

½ large bunch of kale, leaves stripped from the stalks and roughly torn

1 large bunch of callaloo, chopped (or use a couple of handfuls of shredded spring greens or cabbage)

For the dressing

130ml (generous ½ cup) rapeseed (canola) oil

juice of 1 lemon

½ tsp English mustard

3 garlic cloves, peeled

salt and freshly ground black pepper

Heat the oil in a heavy-based wok over a medium heat. Add the chopped chard stalks first and sauté for 1–2 minutes until slightly softened.

Add the kale and sauté for a further few minutes. Add the callaloo or spring greens/cabbage and sauté again for 1–2 minutes.

Lastly, add the chard leaves and sauté until wilted. Use tongs to thoroughly mix all the greens together. Remove from the wok, transfer to a bowl and leave to cool completely.

Meanwhile, to make the dressing, blitz together the oil, lemon juice, mustard, and garlic in a small food processor (alternatively, you can just finely grate the garlic into a bowl and whisk in the rest of the ingredients). Season to taste with salt and pepper. Pour the dressing over the greens and mix it through thoroughly using tongs.

Serve at room temperature.

Sweet potato fritters

Serves 12
Prep time 15 minutes
Cook time 10–15 minutes

Slightly different take on a fritter here, it's a drier mix and I'm using white sweet potato, which I prefer to the pink or orange ones. They have less water, less sugar and I find I get a better, crisper result with them in most dishes. But don't worry if you can't get the white ones, use the others as they ALL work here.

320g (11½oz) white sweet potatoes, peeled and grated

110g (4oz) white onion, grated

4 garlic cloves, finely grated

15g (½oz) fresh ginger, finely grated

1 tsp ground turmeric

1 tsp cumin seeds

1 tsp chilli flakes

40g (generous ¼ cup) self-raising flour

30g (scant ¼ cup) fine cornmeal (polenta)

1 sprig of thyme, leaves only

small bunch of chives, finely chopped

big pinch of salt

big pinch of ground black pepper

500ml (generous 2 cups) neutral oil, such as rapeseed (canola) or sunflower oil, for deep-frying

chopped fresh herbs, chillies and/or spring onions (scallions), to garnish

Combine all the ingredients, apart from the oil and garnish, in a large bowl and mix thoroughly together using your hands. Make sure you really squeeze the mixture so it all sticks together. Cover the bowl with a kitchen towel and set aside for a moment.

Heat the oil in a wide, deep pan to around 150–170°C (300–340°F). To test whether the oil is hot enough, drop in a pinch of the sweet potato mixture. If it rises and starts to go golden quickly, it's ready to fry.

Gently slip 1 level tablespoon of the fritter mixture at a time into the hot oil, trying to keep them a modest size so they'll cook through properly. Fry in batches of 3 or 4 until golden.

Have a plate lined with kitchen paper (paper towels) to one side and transfer the cooked fritters from the pan directly to this using a slotted spoon to drain any excess oil.

Serve the fritters piled high in a bowl and sprinkle over your chosen garnish.

Mum's lemon salted cucumbers

Serves 2–4 as a side
Prep time 5 minutes, plus 15–20 minutes resting

This is how my mum always treated cucumbers. It draws some of the water out and brings out the true flavour. Nice.

½ cucumber, peeled, deseeded, and diced (about 100g/3½oz)

juice of ½ lemon

3½ tbsp good-quality rapeseed (canola) oil

a big pinch of good quality sea salt – I like to use Maldon

a generous pinch of ground black pepper

Combine the diced cucumber, lemon juice, and oil in a bowl with the salt and black pepper. Mix to combine thoroughly, then chill in the fridge for 15–20 minutes before serving.

Cucumber relish

Serves 6–8
Prep time 20 minutes
Cook time 5 minutes

This zingy relish is perfect for bringing freshness to anything rich. It's delicious heaped on top of Doubles (see page 87).

200ml (scant 1 cup) white wine vinegar

4 heaped tbsp white sugar

½ tsp cumin seeds

1 tsp whole white peppercorns

1 bay leaf, roughly torn

70g (2½oz) roughly chopped spring onions (scallions)

6 coriander (cilantro) stalks, roughly chopped

315g (11½oz) finely diced cucumber

pinch of salt

Add the vinegar, sugar, cumin seeds, peppercorns, bay leaf, and 3½ tablespoons of water to a medium saucepan. Warm through over a low heat until the sugar has dissolved, stirring occasionally. Set aside to cool.

Once the liquid is cool, add the spring onions (scallions), coriander (cilantro) stalks, and most of the diced cucumber, reserving about 2 tablespoons.

Give the mixture a stir to combine, then pour into a blender and blitz briefly to a rough consistency. Transfer to a bowl and stir through the reserved diced cucumber. Add a pinch of salt and serve as you like.

Melting white sweet potatoes

Serves 4 as a side
Prep time 10 minutes
Cook time 20–25 minutes

A buttery-soft treatment of one of my favourite vegetables, the white sweet potato. They are less sweet than the orange or pink varieties, firmer and to my mind closer to a parsnip in taste and texture. If you can't get hold of white sweet potato, I would suggest making this with parsnips instead; it will bring you just the right amount of melting, aromatic joy.

2 medium white sweet potatoes

200g (1¾ sticks) unsalted butter, diced

splash of extra virgin rapeseed (canola) oil

2 garlic cloves, peeled and bashed

2 red chillies, finely chopped

2 sprigs of thyme

400ml (1¾ cups) stock of your choice

salt and freshly ground black pepper

Peel the sweet potatoes and cut them into 5-cm (2-in) thick rounds.

Add 2 teaspoons of the butter and a splash of oil to a large sauté pan set over a medium heat. Add the sweet potato rounds, garlic, chillies, and thyme and sauté the sweet potatoes until they have a lovely golden-brown colour on each side.

Now start adding the stock, a ladle at a time, and gradually throw in pieces of the butter every 4–5 minutes. Keep the pan simmering, turning and cooking the potatoes in the stock for about 25 minutes in total, or until they are tender. Finish with some salt and pepper and serve.

Mofongo

Serves 7
Prep time 15–25 minutes
Cook time 10–20 minutes

We can easily forget that Puerto Rico is part of the Caribbean. It has an array of fascinating dishes, which, like all of the region, are a mixture of African, Portuguese, Latin American, and beyond in their influence. I recently discovered mofongo, and it just about blew my mind! You can find versions in Puerto Rico, Dominica, and Cuba too. The dish has ties to Angola in its methodology, where they mash a starch before adding fats and liquid to bring it all together. Clearly this technique is popular around the world – you only have to think of mashed tatties, for example, the best versions of which are packed with butter and cream. The word mofongo comes from the Angolan "mgwenge-mfwenge", which means "a great amount of anything at all", so essentially the vibe is mash up what you can get your hands on and then sex it up.

200g (7oz) pork meat or bacon/pancetta or dry chorizo

neutral oil, such as rapeseed (canola) or sunflower oil, for frying

7 unripe/green plantains or bananas

6 garlic cloves, peeled

2 tbsp good quality extra-virgin olive oil

lime juice, to taste

salt and freshly ground black pepper

2–3 tbsp chopped parsley or coriander (cilantro), to garnish

For the sauce

500ml (generous 2 cups) chicken or pork stock

1 tsp cornflour (corn starch)

First, dice or thinly slice your chosen pork meat. Fry it off in a little neutral oil until crispy, then turn off the heat, remove the meat to a plate and set aside. Leave the fat that has come out of the meat in the pan to make a sauce later.

Next, to prepare the plantain or bananas, top and tail each one, then peel and chop them into equal chunks. Soak them in a bowl of water seasoned with a large pinch of salt for 15 minutes. The salty water will season the plantain or bananas and take away some of the chalkiness. Drain and dry them well using kitchen paper (paper towels).

Heat a generous splash of neutral oil in a heavy-based frying pan over a medium–low heat. When the oil is hot, fry the plantains/bananas for about 10–15 minutes until soft and lightly golden brown. Drain the excess oil on kitchen paper and set aside to cool.

Add the garlic cloves, browned meat and good-quality oil to a large bowl and begin to mash them together using the end of a rolling pin or a pestle. Gradually add the cooked plantain and continue to vigorously mash until everything is thoroughly combined. Season with salt, pepper, and lime juice to taste. Pack individual portions of the mixture into small bowls or dessert moulds and flip onto serving plates.

To make the sauce, put the chicken stock in a saucepan along with the reserved pork cooking fat and let them bubble up over a medium heat. Combine the cornflour (corn starch) with a splash of water in a mug and mix to make a slurry. Whisk the slurry into the stock and continue to heat for a further 5–6 minutes until slightly thickened.

Adjust the seasoning to your taste and pour the sauce over the mofongo to serve. Garnish with parsley or coriander (cilantro) and enjoy immediately.

Cornmeal & cassava

With ingredients like cornmeal and cassava, you can find direct connections to our African mothers and fathers, our ancestors (that African hand I mentioned on page 75). In fact, I discovered the other day that in Angola, they call cornmeal made in a particular way fungee, just like we do in Antigua. I love these connections. It reminds me that I am connected to this HUGE diaspora, and I feel the pride and the love of that coursing through my veins. The way we all use cornmeal AND cassava feels properly ancient; in puddings, pones, porridges, fungee, cou cou, bamboula, and on and on. I can feel the echo of kitchens across the world, frying, pounding, beating and "turning" across the years, and there is something very settling about this – a quieting feeling. Once again when it comes to these two ingredients, you'll find different versions of the heritage recipes right across the Caribbean.

Friday 12th February

Sister Hector & Granny

Tom is here! My friend Tom and I have been taking pictures of the food I make and talking about getting the opportunity to be here in the Caribbean together for about 7 years, and now he's actually here. I'm so excited and can't wait to show him everything. The whole trajectory of this trip seems to be about things finally happening.

Today we went to meet Sister Hector and my friend Charlie's granny, who is just called Granny by everyone. We have JUST got back from our morning with the ladies. First, we spent time with Granny and her granddaughter, the wonderful Charlie, walking her garden and picking leaves, soaking up sunshine and family stories. It turns out the family bought the land that they live on in the 40s/50s, when Charlie's great grandpa got a lift in a horse and buggy from a man driving into town, who happened to be selling it cheap. The family have lived there in one way or another ever since then.

There is one of the biggest mango trees I've ever seen right at the front of the house. It feels like its own place of shelter, of solace. I'm reading a book at the moment called *Their Eyes Were Watching God* by Zora Neale Hurston. In it one of the characters lies under a peach tree, imagining all the paths her life could take; she is on the cusp of possibility. The tree at Granny's house reminds me of that moment in the book, I feel drawn to it. I will come back to see it when it is full of fruit, fecund with ripe mangoes... maybe I'll bring my book and lie underneath it. There is something so romantic about a huge towering old tree, heavy with its ripe gift.

Sister Hector is one of those people who has such sweetness within her. Just being around her makes you feel calm, you know? Tom and I went to visit her fully expecting that we'd spend perhaps half an hour together, and she would tell us about the leaves and branches we'd picked at Granny's, and then we'd leave her in peace. She is bursting with so much knowledge, though, that she can't wait to share it with you.

I asked her about a cornbread dumpling I'd just read about in another book called *To Shoot Hard Labour*, which is a first-person account of post-emancipation, a supposed free and much easier life in Antigua. It's a fascinating, troubling, compelling study and I couldn't put it down. In it the narrator, Papa Sammy, talks about some of the food that people used to cook. He mentions a type of cornbread called cha cha dumpling, which I'd never heard of before, so I've been asking around.

Sister Hector immediately offered to show me how she makes her version, and also how to make a bread from cassava called bamboula, which I had previously only seen in Jamaica in the form of bammy. The Antiguan version she makes has a sweet coconut stuffing, and is like nothing I've tasted before, just delectable. She showed us how she makes cassava flour, AND the by-products from that, which are the straining fibres and cassava starch you can make a porridge from.

My brain is now full, full, full, not to mention my heart. Sister Hector is the most generous, lovely, fascinating, kind woman, with a spatula she made herself from Formica, a handmade grater and a giggle that sets your whole world to rights.

OH MY GOD, I NEARLY FORGOT! She also made these amazing sugar stewed star fruits that she is going to use in her birthday cake next month, when she will be 85. I am obsessed – I've always found star fruit to be pretty boring, but this is alchemy. They're transformed into the most delicious cross between dates and prunes, eliciting a beautiful thick, dark syrup. I think I want them with meat that has crispy caramelized fat...

ON THE MENU TODAY

CASSAVA FRIES

STICKY STAR FRUIT PORK CHOPS

SORREL PUNCH

Cassava fries

Serves 4 as a side
Prep time 15 minutes
Cook time 20 minutes

If you're anything like me, you're always keen to find out about new varieties of fries! Sometimes called yuca fries, cassava fries are satisfyingly starchy in just the right way. This version adds a little turmeric to push the colour and depth of flavour further.

1 cassava

pinch of sugar

pinch of salt, plus extra to serve

1 tsp ground turmeric

200ml (scant 1 cup) oil

neutral oil, such as rapeseed (canola) or sunflower oil, for frying

Peel the cassava, then cut it into chunky sized chips. Cook the cassava in a large saucepan of boiling water, seasoned with the sugar and salt, for about 8–10 minutes until tender. Drain.

In a bowl, mix the turmeric and oil together. Toss the drained cassava in the turmeric oil, then tip onto a wire rack with a tray or plate underneath to catch any drips of oil. Leave to cool slightly.

Heat the oil in a deep-fat fryer or heavy-based saucepan to 180°C (350°F). To test whether the oil is hot enough, drop in a cube of white bread. If it bubbles straight away and goes golden, then the oil is ready for frying. Fry the cassava in batches until they are golden brown on all sides. Remove from the oil with a slotted spoon and place on a plate lined with kitchen paper (paper towels) to drain any excess oil.

Season with more salt to taste and serve. These are particularly lovely with Chocolate Curry Goat (see page 97).

Sticky star fruit pork chops

Serves 2
Prep time 10 minutes
Cook time 2 hours 20 minutes

Crisp, succulent pork meets sticky fruit... it's a story that never gets old, and this time we're using Sister Hector's spiced star fruit. You can buy star fruit in the UK and US in markets and some big supermarkets, but I have found that Conference or Bosc pears make a good substitution if you can't find star fruit (though they do take a little longer to soften). This recipe makes more sticky star fruit than you will need for the pork chops (about 12–15 servings), but it keeps well in the fridge for 3–4 weeks and can be used on any type of grilled, roasted, or barbecued meat, fish, or vegetables.

For the sticky star fruit

10 star fruit, tips and ridges peeled off

500g (2½ cups) caster (superfine) sugar

5 star anise

1 cinnamon stick

1 vanilla pod or 4 drops of vanilla extract

For the pork chops

2 medium pork chops

200ml (scant 1 cup) chicken or pork stock

6 tbsp sticky star fruit

grated zest and juice of 1 orange

2 tbsp unsalted butter

salt and freshly ground black pepper

airtight jar or container

First, make the sticky star fruit. Tip all the ingredients into a pot with about 300ml (1¼ cups) of water. Leave over a VERY low heat to simmer for a couple of hours until the mixture becomes a dark, sticky mass (do keep an eye on it, the first time I did it, I fell asleep and burnt the lot – most distressing!).

Leave to cool, then keep in an airtight jar or container in the fridge and use as desired.

For the pork, preheat the oven to 180°C fan (200°C/400°F/ Gas 6).

Sear the rind of the pork chops in a smoking-hot, heavy-based frying pan to render the fat and get it crispy. Turn the heat down a little, then seal the chops on both sides for a few seconds until golden. Transfer the chops to a baking tray and slip into the preheated oven for 6–7 minutes (I like my chops to still be just blushing pink at the centre). Remove from the oven, transfer the chops to a board and leave to rest.

Meanwhile, put the pork chop pan back over a very low heat, add the stock and let it bubble up for a couple of minutes. Add the sticky star fruits with their syrup and the orange zest and juice. Bubble for a couple of minutes again, then add the butter and season to taste with salt and black pepper. Bubble for 1 final minute, then pour the sticky star fruit over the chops to serve.

Sorrel punch

Makes 1.8 litres (7⅔ cups)
Prep time 10 minutes

Sorrel is what we call red hibiscus in the Caribbean. This drink is delightfully aromatic, with a faint murmur of spices that warm as well as refresh. It's often seen as a celebration drink and is frequently made at Christmas, but I like it all year round.

50g (1¾oz) dried sorrel (hibiscus) petals, or use fresh sorrel petals

1 large cinnamon stick or 3 small cinnamon sticks

5 allspice berries

4 whole cloves or 1 tsp ground cloves

thumb-size piece of fresh ginger, peeled and chopped or grated

2 pieces of orange peel

1.8 litres (7⅔ cups) of boiling water

200ml (scant 1 cup) maple syrup, agave syrup or sugar syrup

juice of 1–2 lemons, to taste

ice, to serve

orange wedges, to serve

Put the sorrel, cinnamon stick(s), allspice, cloves, ginger, and orange peel in a large heatproof bowl. Pour the boiling water into the bowl and leave to steep for at least 1 hour or longer if you prefer a stronger taste.

When cooled, strain off the liquid into a large jug (pitcher) and discard the aromatics. Stir in your chosen sweetener and squeeze in some fresh lemon juice to suit your taste.

Serve the punch in glasses over ice, garnished with orange wedges.

Cha cha dumpling

Makes 12
Prep time 10 minutes
Cook time 10 minutes

I am so thrilled when I am introduced to a recipe that is as old as the hills. Cha cha dumpling are one of those beautiful, simple things that I am so happy to have found. Thank you, Sister Hector! A brand new way with cornmeal and a wonderful new side dish that I am completely seduced by. Try it with barbecue chicken or Hard-Grilled Midweek Curry Fish (see page 197).

450g (3 cups) cornmeal (polenta)

225g (1¾ cups) plain (all-purpose) flour

225g (8oz) grated fresh coconut

2 tsp baking powder

1 tbsp milk

1 tbsp water

white sugar, to taste

pinch of salt

pinch of nutmeg

pinch of mixed spice essence

3–4 banana leaves, cut into roughly 15 x 15cm (6in) pieces, for cooking the dumplings

Mix all the ingredients together in a large bowl with a wooden spoon to make a thick batter. The mixture should be thick enough to hold its shape when you spoon it out.

Working in batches to fit the size of your pan, place the cut banana leaves into a heavy-based frying pan, or roti iron if you have one. Place a spoonful of batter onto each leaf and cover with another leaf. Cook over a medium–low heat for about 2–3 minutes.

Flip each banana leaf package over onto the other side and let it cook for another 2–3 minutes.

When the batter has firmed up and stopped sticking to the leaves, discard the leaves and fry the dumplings until brown on both sides.

Remove from the pan and cook the remaining mixture in the same way. Serve.

Fungee

Serves 5–6
Prep time 60–90 minutes
Cook time 45–60 minutes

Fungee and Antigua are like sister and brother; forever connected. This is one of the staple cornmeal dishes of our island: it's a thick cornmeal porridge akin to polenta, traditionally brought together with an okra onion gravy running through it. Like any dish of this nature, there are a few differing ways to make it, but I think this is the simplest and quickest way. The turning of the fungee (this is what we call it when we toss it in butter or oil in a bowl and make a ball out of it) is easy peasy, I promise, and a LOT of fun. A great one to make with kids!

7 okra, finely chopped

1½ tsp salt

2½ tbsp unsalted butter or good-quality olive oil, plus extra for turning/swirling

300g (2 cups) coarse cornmeal (polenta)

Note to reader

Fungee is a hugely important dish in Antigua and Barbuda. The spelling of the word is a controversial issue. Some insist on spelling it like the plural of fungus – "fungi" – these people are wrong, no matter if they are my aunt and have at least three degrees (by the way, I did not write this bit auntie, Sulaiman did, I am Andi and I am the nice one). The word is "fungee" and that is that. Aka: "coo-coo/cou-cou" (Barbados); "turn-cornmeal" (Jamaica); "ugali" (east Africa: Kenya, Uganda).

Bring 1.5 litres (6¼ cups) of water to the boil in a large saucepan. Add the okra, salt, and butter or oil. Cook the okra for about 10 minutes until just softened.

Use a heatproof jug or ladle to remove 500ml (generous 2 cups) of the cooking water and set aside. Begin to slowly pour the cornmeal into the okra water, stirring all the time with a wooden spoon. Once all the cornmeal and water are combined, cover the pan with a lid, reduce the heat to low and leave to cook for about 5 minutes.

Uncover the pan and stir the mixture constantly now. At this point, the mixture will become difficult to stir because of its thick consistency, but it is important to keep stirring as this will prevent lumps from forming. Pour in more of the reserved okra cooking water as the mixture thickens to avoid it drying out and keep the fungee smooth and loose enough to stir. After 20–30 minutes, the cornmeal should be thoroughly cooked. Remove from the heat and continue to stir for about 5 more minutes, pressing the spoon against the sides of the pan to smooth out any lumps of cornmeal.

Now its time to "turn the fungee". Spoon a teaspoon of butter or oil into a small bowl. Deposit a wooden spoonful of the cooked fungee into the bowl and swirl until it forms a little ball. Set the ball aside and repeat with the remainder of the cooked fungee, adding a teaspoon more butter or oil for every other spoonful.

Serve the fungee immediately alongside Antiguan classics such as Mama's Pepperpot (see page 14), steamed fish, brown-stewed fish or saltfish. Or eat as a breakfast staple along with eggs, sausages, corned beef, etc.

Plantain & coconut fungee

Makes 5–6 small balls
Prep time 10 minutes
Cook time 10–12 minutes

I can already hear all the aunties and uncles up in arms about me putting coconut milk and mashed sweet plantain in fungee. However, I have to say it's seriously one of the best ideas I've ever had!

1 very ripe (dark brown/black) plantain, peeled and roughly chopped

300ml (1¼ cups) stock of your choice

1 x 400ml (13.5fl oz) can of coconut milk

1 tsp Caribbean curry powder

big pinch of coarsely ground black pepper

big pinch of salt

pinch of fresh thyme leaves

300g (scant 2 cups) coarse cornmeal (polenta)

unsalted butter, for turning/swirling

Add all the ingredients, apart from the cornmeal and butter, to a medium saucepan.

Bring to the boil and simmer for about 8–10 minutes until the plantain is tender. Remove from the heat and, using a potato masher or a fork, mash the soft plantain into the cooking liquid.

Return the pan to a medium heat and bring to a gentle simmer. Add the cornmeal in a steady stream, while continuously stirring/beating the mixture. It will quickly come together into a very stiff kind of porridge. Keep beating the mixture for another 2 minutes, then pinch off a little piece and taste to check the texture – it should now be smooth and soft. If it's not, cook and stir for a little longer before checking again. Remove from the heat.

Add a knob of butter and a spoonful of the fungee to a small bowl. Swirl the bowl around, tossing the mixture around the bowl until it forms a smooth ball (don't look for a perfect round result, you just want it to come together). Tip out and repeat with another spoonful of fungee and 1 teaspoon more butter for every other swirl. Serve with any curry, Stout-Braised Oxtail (see page 245), or saltfish or barbecued chicken – whatever you fancy.

Bamboula

Serves 2
Prep time 10 minutes
Cook time 10 minutes

I was introduced to this recipe by Sister Hector, and when I tried it back home in my kitchen and it worked I whooped (yes, whooped!) with excitement. It was like I'd got all A's in my homework (which probably never happened now that I think about it). Bamboula is like bammy with its best dress on, all gussied up and headed to my table... fabuLOUS.

80g (1 generous cup) fresh grated coconut

40g (⅛ cup) dark brown soft sugar

1 tsp good quality vanilla extract

2 tsp good quality dark or light rum

240g (8½oz) peeled and grated cassava (you can shred this in a food processor if you prefer, just cut into small pieces first so that it breaks down properly)

10cm (4in) cooking ring

Add the grated coconut, sugar, vanilla, and rum to a bowl and mix to combine.

Heat a heavy-based frying pan or roti stone over a low heat. Place a 10cm (4in) ring in the middle of the pan or stone and pack 60g (2oz) of the cassava into the bottom.

Next, spoon in 40g (1½ oz) of the coconut sugar mixture, then pack another 60g (2oz) of cassava on top. Press down with the back of a tablespoon and gently cook the stack for about 5 minutes.

Slide a palette knife underneath the ring and carefully flip the whole stack over – it should be golden underneath; if it's not, flip it back and cook for a couple more minutes.

Once turned, leave for a further 5 minutes or so to cook on the other side until deep golden in colour. Slip the ring off the pan or stone and onto a board. Leave to cool for about 10 minutes before removing the ring. Repeat the cooking process with the remaining mixture to make another bamboula.

You can eat the bamboula straight away while still warm, or enjoy later cold.

Mum's banana pancakes

Serves 8
Prep time 5–10 minutes
Cook time 10–15 minutes

You know that moment when you realize the bananas in the fruit bowl are browner than you want them to be, and you're not sure what to do with them? Here is the answer! Whenever my mum comes to stay, she goes through phases of making Antiguan banana pancakes every morning, it's like her settling in ritual. Waking up to the smell of them, I'm immediately 5 years old again. I adore them. They're a bit more like an American pancake rather than a European one, because they're thicker and have a little rise. They're fluffy, full of banana flavour, slightly spiced and deliciously soothing.

There's a strange law of physics which dictates that the first pancake is always rubbish, whether you're making a crepe, an American stack, or one of these quintessentially Antiguan banana ones. I don't know why this is, but don't be discouraged! Just accept it as a cook's treat to nibble on the side and keep going. Make sure you don't have the pan too hot, as I have found that, as in life, patience in the kitchen is always a virtue.

1 large or 2 small overripe bananas (about 200g/7oz peeled weight)

130g (scant 1 cup) self-raising flour

20g (⅛ cup) cornflour (corn starch)

300ml (1¼ cups) milk of any kind

1 tsp baking powder

a big pinch of salt

neutral oil, such as rapeseed (canola) or sunflower oil, for frying

Mash the banana(s) in a deep bowl, then add the rest of the ingredients and beat together with a wooden spoon until evenly combined into a batter. Cover the bowl and leave the batter to rest for 15 minutes.

Add a little splash of oil to a non-stick frying pan set over a low–medium heat. Gently spoon 1 small ladleful of batter into the pan. If you are using a small pan, cook them one at a time, but if you have a large frying pan, you'll be able to make 2 at once.

When bubbles start to form on top of the pancake(s), gently flip over and cook on the other side for a couple of minutes until golden. Remove from the pan and repeat the cooking process, adding more oil if needed, until all the batter has been used. You can keep the cooked pancakes warm by wrapping them in a clean kitchen towel and keeping them next to the stove, if you wish.

Serve the banana pancakes like my mum does, with crispy streaky bacon and a fried egg or a sticky boiled egg and avocado. They are also delicious served with saltfish and avocado or with fresh fruit and cream.

Cornmeal pudding

Serves 8–10
Prep time 20 minutes
Cook time 50 minutes

An inspired use of cornmeal that you will find on most islands, cornmeal pudding is a versatile and delicious dish, residing in that place between sweet and savoury. Have it with barbecued meat, smoked grilled fish, soused pork, or even with crisp streaky bacon and an egg – yes, I know I suggest that a lot don't I? I love the ingenious "soft top" made with coconut milk and sugar.

55g (scant ¼ cup) unsalted butter, plus extra for greasing

1.5 litres (6¼ cups) coconut milk (canned or fresh)

350g (generous 1¾ cups) dark brown soft sugar

1 tsp vanilla extract

2 tsp golden rum

450g (3 cups) fine cornmeal (polenta)

80g (⅔ cup minus 1 tbsp) self-raising flour

¾ tsp salt

1 tsp ground nutmeg

2 tsp ground cinnamon

100g (⅔ cup) raisins or sultanas (optional)

For the soft top

240ml (1 cup) coconut milk

55g (¼ cup) dark brown soft sugar

1 tsp cinnamon

approx. 30 x 25cm/12 x 10in baking tray, greased with butter

Preheat the oven to 180°C fan (200°C/400°F/Gas 6).

Put the coconut milk, butter, brown sugar, and vanilla extract into a saucepan and warm through over a medium–low heat without letting it boil. Heat until the sugar has dissolved, then remove from the heat, mix in the rum and set aside.

Thoroughly combine all the dry ingredients (cornmeal, flour, salt, nutmeg, and cinnamon) in a large mixing bowl. Little by little, gradually pour the warm coconut milk mixture into the dry ingredients, stirring well with each addition. If you are adding raisins, now is the time to throw them in. Mix well one final time, then pour the mixture into the buttered tray.

Slip into the preheated oven and bake for 25 minutes. Whilst that is happening, mix together the ingredients to make the soft top in a separate bowl.

Remove the pudding from the oven, it will be three-quarters cooked. Pour the soft top mixture over it, then bake for a further 15 minutes. The bottom will be set with a lovely, silky soft top finish.

You can eat the pudding just like this with some cream as a sweet dish, OR combine it with salty and savoury things like bacon or sausages as an addition to a gorgeous brunch or try my version of the classic with Pork Belly Souse (see page 242).

Bammy

Makes 8–10
Prep time 15–30 mins
Cook time 15–20 mins

A bammy is a revelation. It's made from grated pressed cassava and seems to hold itself together through sheer force of will. Traditionally it's eaten with fried fish, and when you try the two together you will understand why. Both crisp and firm, yet yielding all at once, the bammy and the fried fish are firm friends. The history of the bammy goes way back. It was eaten by the Arawaks, one of the original inhabitants of Jamaica, and I'm pretty sure this recipe has never changed. If it ain't broke, etc, etc.

1kg (2¼lb) good-quality, sweet ripe cassava

salt, to taste

neutral oil, such as rapeseed (canola) or sunflower oil, for frying

800ml (3⅓ cups) organic coconut milk

muslin cloth (cheesecloth)

tortilla press or 10cm (4in) baking ring (optional)

To begin, peel the cassava and then grate it on the fine side of a box grater. Place the grated cassava in a muslin cloth and wring out the liquid until most of it has drained, leaving the cassava just a little bit moist.

Place the cassava in a bowl, season with salt to taste and mix well.

Heat a drizzle of oil in a cast-iron pan or non-stick heavy-based pan over a low-medium heat.

Take about 150–250g (5½ –9oz) of the cassava mixture and using your hands, a tortilla press, or a baking ring, shape the mixture into thin discs, about 10–15cm (4–6in) in diameter and about 2–3cm (¾ –1¼ in) thick.

Place a disc in the hot pan and fry for about 5 minutes on each side – being very careful when flipping due to the delicate consistency of the bammy – until just cooked. Repeat for the remaining discs, using more oil in the pan as needed.

Leave the bammies to cool, then chill in the fridge for a minimum of 30 minutes (or freeze for later consumption).

Just before you are ready to eat, soak the bammies in the coconut milk for up to 10 minutes (or less time if the breads are not very thick).

Once soaked, refry the breads in a little more oil over a medium–high heat until perfectly golden brown; this shouldn't take more than a few minutes on each side. Serve immediately and enjoy hot as a snack or side dish with soup or stew, or fill with meat, veg, or fish of your choice.

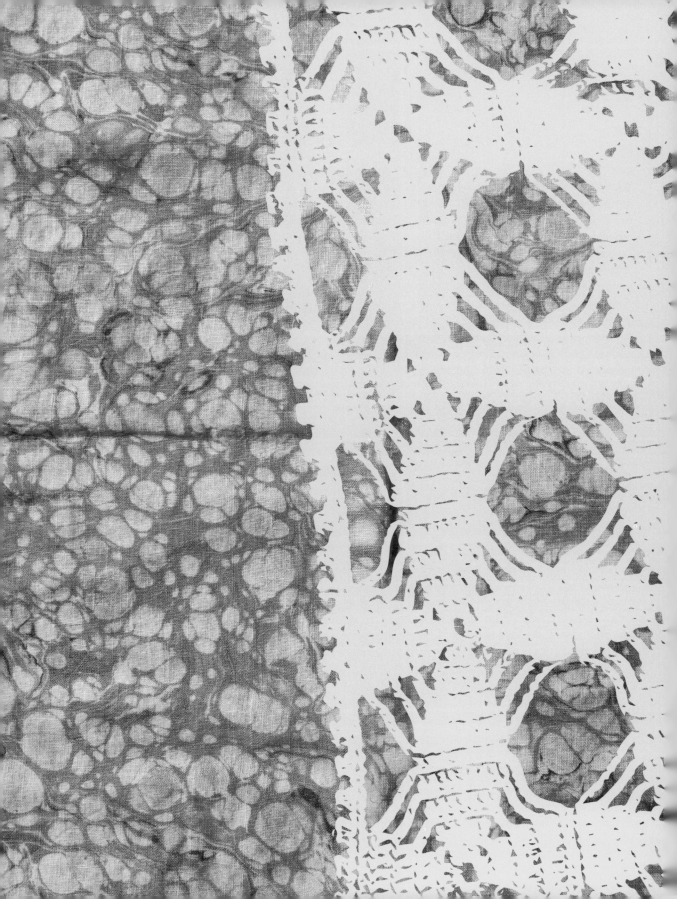

Ital is vital

Cooking with vegetables is intrinsic to a Caribbean table. There is such a wealth of produce to work with, and in the old days most people couldn't afford to eat much meat anyway.

You will still find a huge array of vegetable and pulse dishes in any Caribbean feast, sometimes with a little meat running through them for flavour, but oftentimes they contain no meat, fish, or even dairy at all. This is ital.

Ital food has been around for decades. It's the Rastafarian way of cooking healthily and living with the land and spirit. No meat, fish, dairy, chemicals, or alcohol. But it's about more than what is or isn't on the plate for Rastafarians, it is a spiritual way of life. The idea that veganism is a new, Western concept is actually something of nonsense. In the Caribbean, it's a way of cooking that has been around for generations.

There is a whole movement amongst cooks from the African diaspora who are cooking ital food, and when it's good, it's reeeally good. The wealth of herbs and spices typically found in the Caribbean larder work beautifully to create depth and layers of flavour. For us, ital is about bringing out the natural beauty of the pure produce.

Digestive health is something that has always been focused on in our culture. The idea for what we call a "cleanout" is a very, very old one. In the Western diet market, this is sold as a "detox", with expensive supplements and sometimes dubious promises of life-changing health benefits. When I was a kid, Mum used to put us on a juice day once a month, where we would only have vegetable and fruit juices and loads of water – a "cleanout". I, of course, found this massively embarrassing if one of my white English mates came round and all there was for tea was juice. They thought we were REALLY odd. Now, I'm quite proud of her for following her own path.

Saturday 13th February

Market day is the best day of all

It's market day tomorrow, yay!! I've been waiting for Tom to get here so we could take pictures at the same time. We'll have to get up at 5am, because if you don't get there by 6am you miss all the best stuff! I'm so excited I'm not sure I'll be able to sleep...

In the end we got up at 4:30am. Markets are my favourite places in the world, and the St. John's market is just a hustle and bustle of complete glory. I am so proud of myself, though, I have a terrible propensity to over shop, and yet I managed to control myself in the face of the most stunning bounty. It could be that the eyes of Tom Mattey on me made me rein myself in (although he usually has the opposite effect, actually, ask anyone who knows us), but I'd like to believe it's because I have learnt some self-restraint.

I found things I'd never seen before, like long beans that remind me of those Asian long green beans, which I didn't know we had here in the Caribbean. Things I dimly recall hearing about from childhood, like cassie which is essentially the paddle of a cactus leaf with the spikes taken out, then peeled at the edges and thinly sliced (for me, it's a bit like a cross between asparagus and okra). I saw a bush tea lady and stocked up on some dandelion, lemongrass, a type of mint, some noni balsam, Christmas bush, French thyme and soursop tea. I will make tea, put some leaves in a brine for my fish or chicken, and add some to my green seasoning. I also bought fresh pigeon peas to cook for dinner tonight. We found a lady making the wonderful bamboula that Sister Hector introduced us to yesterday, and she had cha cha dumpling wrapped in sea grape leaves on the grill too. Another morning of Andi heaven.

The market is packed full and bustling, but like a lot of things in Antigua, everyone is so mannerly. Lots of "Yes honey", "Good morning my dear", "Thank you darling". It was a good job we went early, though, because the crowd was still manageable then. I'm pretty sure that some of those manners dissipated after a while, because when we left at about 8am it was getting BUUUSSSY and HOT and showed no signs of slowing down.

ON THE MENU TODAY

ACKEE & CHARRED CORN PURÉE

SPRING VEGETABLES & GUNGO PEAS

SPICED ROAST GROUND PROVISION

Ackee & charred corn purée

Serves 8 as a side
Prep time 15 minutes
Cook time 30 minutes

I've just had a lovely chat with the wonderful chef Adejoke of West African restaurant Chishuru, based in Brixton. Adejoke is so inspiring and joyful, and I just love to talk to her about food. She described one of the things that we are both interested in as bringing the old and the new world together, which to me is a perfectly succinct way of describing what lures me back to the kitchen again and again. This purée is a great expression of that thought. Creamed corn, but not as you know it. Inviting and luxurious but incredibly easy to make.

Ackee is a peculiar not-sweet fruit that some of you will already be familiar with. It's often served with saltfish and fried dumplings. I recently discovered that when creamed together with sweetcorn, it creates the most velvety thing of beauty. Two of my favourite things; something simple made special and incredibly easy. A double win!

1 x 200g (7oz) can of sweetcorn, drained

1 x 280g (10oz) can of ackee, drained

250ml (1 cup plus 1 tbsp) oat cream or another plant-based cream of your choice

salt and freshly ground black pepper

blender

Add the sweetcorn kernels to a non-stick frying pan and gently toast them over a medium–low heat for around 8–10 minutes, stirring often, until they become slightly charred.

Add the ackee to the pan and fry for 1–2 minutes, mixing them both together.

Now put your ackee and corn into a blender with the oat cream and blitz until smooth.

Stand a sieve over a bowl and push the mixture through it using the back of a spoon (this is not essential but it will give you a silkier end result). Season the purée with salt and pepper to taste.

Spring vegetables & gungo peas

Serves 4–6 as a side
Prep time 15 minutes
Cook time 20 minutes

Gungo peas, sometimes called pigeon peas or "field peas" in Southern American soul food, are a favourite thing of mine. Nutty and almost sweet in flavour, they act as the welcoming anchor in a pot of food. This is an ital dish, light and gorgeous and perfect for the springtime table.

1 small bunch of asparagus

rapeseed (canola) oil, for frying

2 banana shallots, finely chopped

3 garlic cloves, finely grated

½ tsp cumin seeds

½ tsp coriander seeds

about 400ml (1¾ cups) vegetable stock

½ tsp English mustard or mustard of your choice

220g (8oz) drained canned cooked gungo peas

1 tbsp unsalted plant-based butter

grated zest and juice of 1 lemon

1 courgette (zucchini), sliced into rounds

handful of sugar snap peas, cut into bite-sized pieces

handful of okra, roughly chopped

200g (7oz) spinach or callaloo

salt and freshly ground black pepper

Remove the woody ends from the asparagus and trim the spears in half, separating the bottoms and tips. Set aside.

Set a large sauté pan over a medium heat with a splash of oil. Cook the shallots and garlic for 5 minutes over a medium–low heat until translucent.

Add the cumin and coriander seeds and toast for 1 minute. Pour in the vegetable stock, mustard, and gungo peas and simmer for 2–3 minutes. Add the butter and half of the lemon zest and juice. Season with salt and pepper and set aside.

Add another splash of oil to a separate large pan, and sauté the asparagus bottoms for a few minutes, before adding the courgette (zucchini) and a pinch of salt. When the courgette starts to soften and take on a little golden colour, add the sugar snap peas, asparagus tips, okra, and spinach. Pour over the warm stock and beans, give everything a good stir and serve immediately with the remaining lemon zest and juice.

Spiced roast ground provision

Serves 4
Prep time 15 minutes
Cook time 45 minutes

Ground provisions are exactly what they say... that which the ground provides. Sometimes they're also called "hard food" on a Caribbean table. It strikes me that in the Caribbean, I would use yam, sweet potato, cassava, pumpkin, or whatever was in season, and so the same should apply when here or anywhere else. The vegetables I've used in this recipe were readily available to me, but if you can't get any of these, then use whatever you can get your hands on and whatever is in season (carrot, parsnip, squash, potato... you get the picture) and treat them as I have in this dish.

For the spiced ground provision

975g (scant 2¼lb) mixed seasonal root vegetables (I used carrot, swede/rutabaga, sweet potato, and parsnip), diced into roughly 5cm (2in) pieces

big pinch of sea salt flakes

½ tsp ground black pepper

1 tsp ground allspice

1 tsp ground turmeric

1 tsp cayenne pepper

225g (8oz) baby spinach leaves

For the onion and garlic purée

¼ onion, finely chopped

4 garlic cloves

1⅓ tbsp rapeseed (canola) oil

food processor

Preheat the oven to 200°C fan (220°C/425°F/Gas 7).

First, make the onion and garlic purée by blitzing the onion and garlic together with the oil in a food processor.

Tip the root vegetables into a large bowl with the salt, pepper, spices, and onion and garlic purée and mix really well.

Evenly spread the vegetables out in a baking tray. Roast in the preheated oven for 40–45 minutes, tossing halfway through, until the vegetables are tender and golden.

Remove the tray of veg from the oven and tip it into a large saucepan set over a low heat. Add the spinach and stir gently until the spinach is slightly wilted. Serve.

Pumpkin & plantain coconut curry

Serves 6
Prep time 15 minutes
Cook time 1 hour

Warming, quick, and delivering on BIG flavour, this one is a midweek must!

neutral oil, such as rapeseed (canola) or sunflower oil, for frying

1 onion, thinly sliced

2 tbsp Green Seasoning (see page 110)

1 cinnamon stick

1 tsp cumin seeds

1 tbsp Caribbean curry powder

½ tsp ground turmeric

1 Scotch bonnet, very finely chopped

600g (1lb 5oz) pumpkin, peeled, deseeded, and diced

200g (generous 1 cup) dried split red lentils, washed

600ml (2½ cups) vegetable or chicken stock

2 ripe plantains

250ml (1 cup plus 1 tbsp) coconut milk

400g (7 cups) roughly chopped spinach

Pour a splash of oil into a high sided frying pan or wok with a lid and set over a medium–low heat. Add the onion and fry for around 15 minutes until softened. Add the green seasoning, cinnamon stick, cumin seeds, and curry powder and fry off for a couple of minutes before adding the turmeric and chilli.

Add the pumpkin and lentils and stir to combine with the onion and spices. Pour in the stock, pop the lid on the pan and cook over a low heat for 30 minutes, or until the pumpkin is tender and the lentils are nearly cooked.

Meanwhile, peel, slice, and fry the plantain in a splash of oil in a separate pan until golden on each side. Set aside.

Add the coconut milk and most of the fried plantain to the curry (saving some for the garnish) and give it all a good stir. Lay the chopped spinach over the top of the curry in the pan and cook for a further 10 minutes.

Finally, gently stir through the wilted spinach and serve the curry garnished with the remaining fried plantain, alongside the rice or bread of your choice.

Loaded ital beans

Serves 4–6
Prep time overnight soaking
Cook time 2 hours 20 minutes

For the black-eyed beans

500g (generous 3 cups) dried black-eyed beans (black-eyed peas; or other beans of your choice)

1 whole garlic bulb, cut in half widthways

1 onion, roughly chopped

1 whole chilli

small handful of dried mushrooms

3 small bay leaves

1 cinnamon stick

2 star anise

20g (¾oz) thumb of fresh ginger

4 whole green cardamom pods

2 tbsp molasses

2 tbsp soy sauce

2 tsp tamarind concentrate

salt and freshly ground black pepper

For the roast ground provisions (see Note)

1 sweet potato, peeled and cut into small cubes (peel reserved)

2 carrots, peeled and cut into small cubes (peel reserved)

2 eddoes, peeled and cut into small cubes (peel reserved)

2 plantains, peeled and sliced (peel reserved)

salt and freshly ground black pepper

For the broth (or use vegetable stock)

ground provisions vegetable peelings

2 garlic cloves, peeled

1 onion, halved

handful of mixed dried mushrooms of your choice

1 chilli of your choice

1 sprig of thyme

I love a pot of beans as much as the next person, but it can get boring. I've loaded these up with glorious roasted roots to bring some new texture and liven up the proceedings!

The night before cooking, soak the black-eyed beans in 1 litre (4⅓ cups) cold water. Leave in the fridge overnight.

If you are making the peelings broth, peel and chop the veggies the night before (keeping the prepared veggies in the fridge) and tip all the peelings into a medium saucepan along with the rest of the broth ingredients. Cover with water and simmer gently for about 1 hour. Strain the broth through a sieve and keep in the fridge to use the next day.

The next day, drain the soaked beans and tip them into a large pot. Cover with 2 litres (8½ cups) of fresh water. Add the garlic bulb, onion, chilli, dried mushrooms, bay leaves, cinnamon stick, star anise, ginger, and green cardamom pods. Gently bubble over a medium heat for about 1 hour, or until the beans are tender (note that if you are using a different pulse cooking times will vary).

Meanwhile, preheat the oven to 150°C fan (170°C/340°F/Gas 4).

Combine all the peeled and chopped ground provision vegetables and plantain in a baking tray. Season with salt and pepper and roast in the preheated oven for about 40 minutes until golden and tender. Leave to one side.

After 1 hour, give the pot of beans a good stir. Remove the big knob of ginger, the thyme stalks, and any woody bits from the garlic bulb if you desire. Add the molasses, soy sauce, and tamarind. There should still be some liquid in the pot with the beans, but to keep the consistency flowing, add a couple of ladles of peelings broth or vegetable stock (any leftover broth can be used in a multitude of ways!).

Add the ground provisions and plantain to the pot of beans and simmer for 15 minutes. Season to taste again and serve.

Note to reader

Use anything you like for the roast ground provisions, i.e.
– whatever the ground provides! Parsnips, potatoes,
Jerusalem artichokes, celeriac, etc. all work.

Leek & callaloo

Serves 4 as a side
Prep time 15 minutes
Cook time 10 minutes

The verdant nature of leeks means they make a great addition to a pan of callaloo. This is a moreish vegetable side dish, and SO nutritious.

2 tbsp cold pressed rapeseed (canola) oil

4 garlic cloves, grated

2 small leeks, thinly sliced

2 big handfuls of spring greens, or dark green cabbage or kale, thinly shredded

5 bunches (1 large bag) callaloo or spinach, stalks removed

1½ tbsp unsalted butter (or vegan butter)

salt and freshly ground black pepper

Add the oil and garlic to a pan over a medium–low heat and fry the garlic for a few minutes until softened.

Add the leeks and gently cook for 3–4 minutes, then add the hardest greens first (the spring greens, cabbage, or kale). Sauté for a few minutes until they start to soften.

Pile the callaloo or spinach on top, cover the pan and cook for around 3–4 minutes until wilted. Stir the wilted greens through, add the butter and season to taste with salt and black pepper. Serve piping hot.

This is particularly delicious served on top of the Caramelized Onion & Pumpkin Porridge (see page 184).

Curried
carrot scones

Makes 12
Prep time 15 minutes
Cook time 20 minutes

60g (⅓ cup) raisins

3½ tbsp dark rum

450g (scant 3½ cups) self-raising flour,
    plus extra for dusting

2 pinches of salt

1 generous tsp caster or coconut sugar

2 tsp Caribbean curry powder

1 tsp mustard powder

2 tsp baking powder

100g (scant ½ cup) plant-based spread
    or vegan butter

1 carrot, grated (approx. 80g/2¾oz
    grated carrot)

200ml (scant 1 cup) coconut milk

big pinch of fine cornmeal (polenta),
    for dusting

For the sauce

70ml (⅓ cup) coconut milk

1 tsp plant-based spread or vegan butter

2 bird's-eye chillies, thinly sliced

3 tsp white or light brown sugar of
    your choice

little pinch of salt

6cm (2½in) cookie cutter

The inspiration for this one comes from the brilliant baker, Bee Rawlinson. I was gazing at a post of hers on a Facebook group that I have long been a member of, run by the absolute genius man that is Marky Souter, AKA the Porky Punk. It's a place where like-minded cooks can share recipes and food obsessions. I've made many friends there and I love it... long may it last!

Anyway, I digress, I was staring at a picture of Bee's towering golden scones, wondering how on EARTH she got such beautiful layering and height, so I messaged her and got her method. I then started to play around with my own versions... and this is where I landed. Carroty goodness with a sauce on the side that I could happily dip most anything into. And YES, they are ital (plant-based).

Soak the raisins in the rum for 1–2 hours, then drain and roughly chop.

Preheat the oven to 190°C fan (210°C/410°F/Gas 6).

Add the flour, salt, sugar, curry powder, mustard powder, and baking powder to a mixing bowl. Add the spread or butter and mix in using your fingers until you have the texture of crumbs.

Add the carrot and run it through thoroughly again using your fingers, then add the raisins and mix again. Add the coconut milk and bring it all together to make a soft dough.

Dust a board with a pinch of flour and the cornmeal and tip the dough out onto it. Gently bring together with your hands – it's important not to overwork the dough, so go gently. Using a rolling pin, roll out the dough to a thickness of 4cm (1½ in). Using the cookie cutter, stamp out 12 rounds of dough, then transfer them to a greased or non-stick baking tray and set aside. You may need to re-roll scraps of dough to get 12.

Add all the sauce ingredients to a small saucepan and bubble together over a low heat for about 6–7 minutes until you have a lovely silky sauce.

Brush a tiny bit of the sauce over each scone, leaving the chillies and some sauce behind in the pan for garnish. Slip the tray into the preheated oven and bake for about 20 minutes, until the scones are golden brown on top. If you tap the bottom of one it should sound hollow when they are done.

Remove from the oven and brush each scone with the remainder of the sauce, then top each with 1–2 pieces of the sliced chillies left in the pan. Feel free to double the amount of sauce so that you also have some to dunk the scones in! Serve.

Sweet potato pudding

Serves 8
Prep time 45 minutes
Cook time 1 hour 45 minutes

1kg (2¼lb) peeled and grated raw white sweet potato (if you can't find white, using pink or orange sweet potatoes is fine)

120ml (½ cup) coconut milk, evaporated milk, or whole dairy milk (or use a mixture of all 3)

200g (1 packed cup) muscovado or dark brown soft sugar

1 tsp vanilla seeds from a pod, or good quality vanilla extract

3 tbsp unsalted butter, softened

100ml (generous ⅓ cup) dark or spiced rum

2 eggs

grated zest and juice of 1 lime

275g (2 cups) plain (all-purpose) flour

½ tsp ground cinnamon

½ tsp ground nutmeg

½ tsp ground ginger

½ tsp ground allspice

good pinch of salt

2 tsp baking powder

75g (½ cup) fine cornmeal (polenta)

For the soft top

240ml (1 cup) coconut milk

55g (generous ¼ cup) muscovado or dark brown soft sugar

1 tsp ground cinnamon

20–22cm (8–9in) loaf or cake tin

Sometimes called pone, just like the cornmeal version this pudding can be eaten as a dessert or alongside a whole host of savoury dishes. Made with coconut milk in the same way, I'm not sure I can choose between this or the cornmeal version as they're both so delicious, so please don't make me!!

Preheat the oven to 170°C fan (190°C/375°F/Gas 5). Grease your cake tin with butter and set aside.

In a large mixing bowl, combine the grated sweet potato with the milk, sugar, vanilla, butter, rum, eggs, and lime juice and zest. Mix until evenly combined.

Next, add the flour, spices, salt, baking powder, and cornmeal. Mix until thoroughly combined, then pour into the greased cake tin and spread the top even. Slip into the centre of the preheated oven and bake for about 1 hour 30 minutes.

The pudding should be almost cooked at this point – you can check by poking a skewer into the middle; it should come out clean. If it isn't, just return the pudding to the oven for a further 10 minutes or so.

Now it's time for the soft top. Mix the coconut milk, sugar, and cinnamon together and pour over the pudding, slipping the whole thing back into the oven for a final 10 minutes. Serve hot or cold, straight out of the tin or on a board.

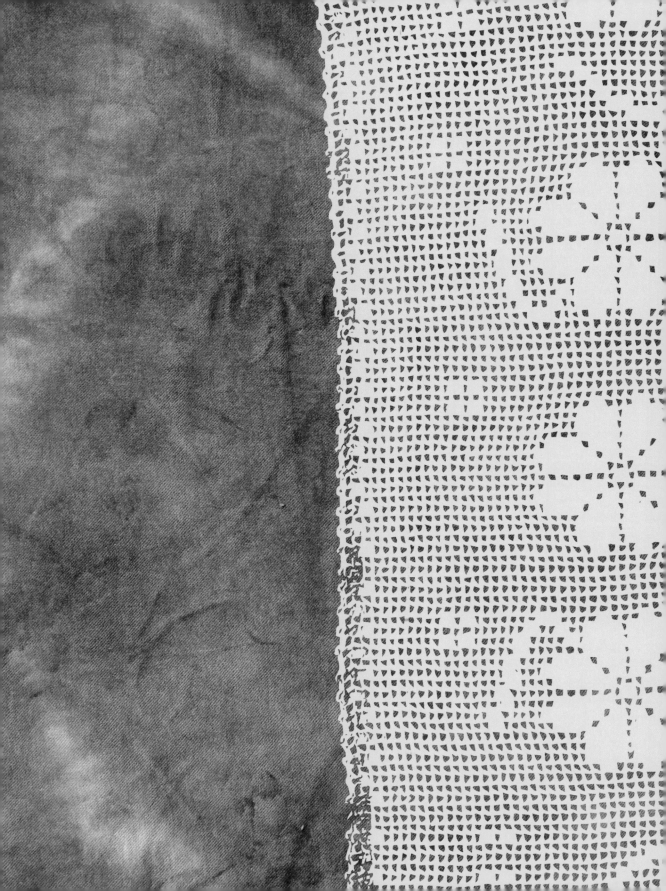

Everyday cooking

Life is just BUSY, right? I know that sometimes I get home and I'm fit to drop, but there is still food to get to the table and a family to feed. Yes, food is my job, but I am very controlling in the kitchen (big shocker, I know) so cooking at home also comes down to me most of the time, because that's the way I like it.

I have a few things in my fridge all the time that help me to get good, full-flavoured food to the table quickly and without too much faff. Things like the ubiquitous green seasoning, a chilli paste here, a jar of curry mix there. These, as any cook will tell you, are an important part of the daily arsenal. From quick stews and light curries, to flash fried or quickly grilled offerings, this next chapter is all about dishes that use delicious Caribbean ingredients in ways that are snappy and don't take a whole lot of time to prepare.

Wednesday 17th February

Work, work, work

It seems that wherever I am in the world, I manage to make myself hectic. I've created a schedule here... a schedule?? I mean, what is wrong with me. I get up at 7am, leave for the gym at 7:45am, class at 8:15am, shopping on the way back, then writing, cooking, or working on our new Wadadli Kitchen project. Just HECTIC!

But I have to say I am SO excited about this new project. We seek to create new conversations between the UK, Africa, the Americas, and the Caribbean in a project of culinary cultural exchange along the old slave trading routes. Instead of trading in pain, bodies, and suffering, we will be creating light, power, and beauty and honouring those who have come before us. I want to work towards giving them back part of that which was robbed from them, their names and their dignity by exploring the art and beauty in soul food pathways. Our diaspora story is one of survival, passion, endurance, power, pain, love, life, and pride. We have been meeting with Karen-Mae Hill, the wonderful High Commissioner in Antigua, to speak about how we can facilitate this idea.

Wadadli Kitchen really is like stepping into my own power and dreams. I feel like something has led me to come here to work. This project is leading me to look at food from right across the Caribbean, including Puerto Rico, Santo Domingo and even parts of Mexico. The places that we sometimes forget are also kissed by the Caribbean sea.

I've been reading about a dish called mofongo, which is a Puerto Rican or Dominican dish of mashed green plantain with pork, herbs, and garlic running through it, traditionally served with a rich broth. Because I can't be bothered to go out to the shops, and also because I have promised to stop running myself ragged, I am going to use what I already have in the fridge to make a version of it. We all know this way of cooking is best practice anyway, and some of my favourite dishes have come about in this way. Hmmm, I seem to have pumpkin, oats, onions, and stock. Let's see where that gets us shall we? It won't be mofongo, but I reckon it's a good launch pad for a quick dinner... this is a kitchen inventing day.

ON THE MENU TODAY

CARAMELIZED ONION & PUMPKIN PORRIDGE

CUCUMBER, GINGER, & LIME JUICE

Caramelized onion & pumpkin porridge

Serves 2
Prep time 10 minutes
Cook time 40 minutes

This may seem an odd entry, but porridge of ALL kinds is big in the Caribbean. Maybe that's why, when I discovered a recipe for an old Scottish dish called skirlie (a type of savoury porridge), I felt a real affinity with it and my imagination just ran wild. I've made many versions of this dish depending on what's available to me at the time. I made one recently with garlicky mushrooms and edamame beans (glorious!). I also like to zap it with a delicious turmeric ghee to finish it off. Pumpkin is a beloved vegetable in the Caribbean, so although this porridge may not be traditional, I feel it's got Caribbean richness and invention at its very heart.

3 tbsp olive oil

2 tsp Caribbean curry powder

½ tsp chilli flakes

200g (7oz) pumpkin or squash, peeled, deseeded and diced into 1cm (½in) pieces

1 onion, thinly sliced

2 garlic cloves, finely grated

3 tsp unsalted butter

100g (scant 1 cup) rolled porridge oats (old fashioned rolled oats)

350–400ml (1½–1¾ cups) chicken stock

salt, to taste

Toppings to serve

store-bought crispy onions

mixed chopped herbs

grated Parmesan

Preheat the oven to 170°C fan (190°C/375°F/Gas 5).

Tip half of the oil, the curry powder, and chilli flakes into a medium bowl and mix into a paste. Add the diced pumpkin to the bowl and stir through to make sure all the pumpkin is thoroughly coated.

Slip the coated pumpkin into an ovenproof dish or onto a baking tray and roast in the preheated oven for about 35 minutes until tender with some bite left.

Meanwhile, gently sauté the onions and garlic in 2 teaspoons of the butter and the remaining oil over a very low heat until soft, sticky, and golden; this will take around 20 minutes.

Remove the pumpkin from the oven and scrape three-quarters of it into the pan with the onion and garlic, keeping the rest for garnish. Give it a good stir.

Now add the oats and stir again to combine everything thoroughly. Pour the chicken stock into the pan and let it all bubble up over a medium heat for around 5 minutes until the oats are cooked. Throw in the remaining teaspoon of butter to finish. Season to taste with salt and serve straight away with your favourite toppings.

Cucumber, ginger, & lime juice

Serves 4
Prep time 10 minutes

When we were in Antigua for a few months, we found the most amazing outside gym. Keep Fit Antigua is run by the wonderful Ellis, who is both heaven and hell all in one man!! On the way back I always stop at the roadside juice lady who makes the BEST juice, just glorious! The most refreshing and perfect thirst quencher for just after a huge workout is this cucumber, ginger, and lime juice.

1 cucumber, roughly chopped

30g (1oz) fresh ginger, peeled and
   roughly chopped

3 pieces of preserved stem ginger in syrup,
   plus 2 tsp of the syrup

juice of 1 lime

1 avocado, halved, pitted, and flesh scooped
   out (optional, but this adds a nice
   creaminess)

big handful of ice, plus extra to serve

blender

Add all the ingredients to a blender with 500ml (generous 2 cups) water and blitz.

Pour the liquid over a sieve to catch any bits. Pour into glasses over ice to serve.

Golden eddoes

Serves 6
Prep time 30 minutes, plus cooling
Cook time 65 minutes

Oh Lord, an eddoe is a thing of great wonder. A bit like a cross between a potato (or Irish potato as it's called in the Caribbean) and a yam, I guess? It's a little starchier than a potato, but you treat it the same way. Usually, we have them boiled as a side dish on a plate of hard food or ground provision, but here I've used a roast potato method and added some spice and, yep, I LOVE it. Of course, if you can't get hold of an eddoe, try this with potatoes instead!

12 eddoes (or new potatoes if you can't get eddoes)

1 x 400ml (13.5fl oz) can of coconut milk

1 tsp ground turmeric

1 whole bird's-eye chilli

2 garlic cloves, peeled

2 bay leaves

200ml (scant 1 cup) chicken or vegetable stock

salt, to taste

generous glug of extra virgin rapeseed (canola) oil

300g (10oz) pumpkin, peeled, deseeded, and cut to the same size as the eddoes (roast potato size)

grated zest of 1 lime, to serve

Peel the eddoes and chop them into pieces roughly the size of roast potatoes. Add the eddoes, coconut milk, turmeric, whole chilli, garlic, bay leaves, stock, and salt to a large, deep saucepan. Simmer for around 25 minutes until the eddoes are tender.

Remove the eddoes from the poaching liquid and keep the pan of cooking liquid to one side. Transfer the eddoes to a bowl and toss them roughly so that the edges get bashed – treat them like you would a parboiled potato that is destined for roasting. Lay them out on a cooling rack and, once cold, leave in the fridge until chilled.

Preheat the oven to 200°C fan (220°C/425°F/Gas 7). Put a roasting tray with a generous glug of extra virgin rapeseed (canola) oil in the oven to heat up.

When the oil is hot, slip the cold eddoes and chopped pumpkin into the roasting tray and return to the oven for around 45 minutes, turning every now and again, until crisp and golden.

Whilst the vegetables are roasting, return to your poaching liquid. Mash any remaining bits of garlic and remove the bay leaves and the whole chilli. Bubble up the poaching stock over a medium–high heat until reduced by a third.

Serve the roasted eddoes and pumpkin in a large bowl with the reduced liquid poured over the top. Scatter over the lime zest to finish.

4-day every which way soup broth

Makes 1–2 servings per day
Prep time 10 minutes here and there over a few days
Cook time 3 hours on day 1
     1 hour 20 minutes on day 2
     20 minutes on day 3
     15 minutes on day 4

Like most people these days, I am always thinking about ways to avoid wasting food, how to use up what I already have and get the best out of the ingredients. The main idea with this soup is that we are using up all those veggies which may have otherwise ended up in the bin. I like to use a mixture of root vegetables that bring different elements to the broth... the carrots and parsnips bring a little sweetness, the potato adds body to the pot, and the alliums bring a different sweetness and a brightness to round out the flavour. However, this really is a do what you like party – so please use whatever vegetables you have in or whatever makes you truly happy.

Whilst I love a weekend blowout with my family and friends, it can mean that the first half of the next week I feel a bit slow and slightly on the back foot. I came up with this soup not only as a way of using up leftovers, but also as a way of recharging my body throughout the week. It really works a treat for me – it's nutritious and full of flavour without being spartan. Because life is too short for depressing food!

Day 1

1 roast chicken carcass, broken up into pieces

leftover roast potatoes from your Sunday roast (whatever you have left, or see Note to reader)

1 whole garlic bulb, peeled but cloves left whole

2 onions, roughly chopped

2 long chillies, or 1–2 Scotch bonnets if you like a good, hot kick

1 heaped tsp Green Seasoning (see page 110)

2 carrots, roughly chopped

1 leek, roughly chopped

1 parsnip, roughly chopped

Take your biggest, deepest pot and add the chicken carcass and all the other ingredients.

Cover the whole lot with 1.5 litres (6¼ cups) cold water and simmer over a medium–low heat for around 3 hours.

Keep an eye on the soup and ensure the liquid level in the pot stays nice and high, covering the ingredients. Keep a jug or cup of water next to the hob (stove) and top up the water with a small splash every time you think the liquid level is getting too low. This will form the base of your soup broth for the next few days. Of course, this is your first day's soup, so serve yourself a big, steaming bowlful.

Leave to cool, then cover and refrigerate overnight.

Continued overleaf

Day 2

2kg (4½lb) chicken wings, cut in half at the joint

2½ tbsp ground allspice

¼ tbsp ground cumin

¼ tsp ground turmeric

2 tbsp Green Seasoning (see page 110)

2 sprigs of thyme

salt and freshly ground black pepper

Lemon & Garlic Dressed Callaloo (see page 125),
    to serve

1 lemon, cut into wedges, to serve

On day 2, preheat the oven to 160°C fan
(180°C/350°F/Gas 4).

Put the chicken wings in a bowl with all the rest of
the day 2 ingredients and mix well. Tip the seasoned
chicken wings out onto 1–2 large baking trays and
spread them out well. Slip into the preheated oven
and roast for about 1 hour until golden.

Add 400ml (1¾ cups) of water and bring your big
pot of soup back to the boil. Pour the cooking liquid
from the roasted chicken wings into the soup. Simmer
for around 15–20 minutes over a medium heat.

To serve, ladle some soup and vegetables into bowls.
Add 3–4 chicken wing pieces to each bowl and top
with some Lemon & Garlic Dressed Callaloo and a
squeeze of fresh lemon juice. Delish!

Leave to cool, then save the rest of the soup and the
wings in separate containers in the fridge overnight.

Day 3

1 plantain, cut into even slices

1 sweet potato, peeled and diced

1 chunk of pumpkin (about 200g/7oz), peeled
    and diced

On day 3, add all the day 3 ingredients to
the big soup pot along with 400ml (1¾ cups) water.

Bring to the boil, then simmer for about 15–20
minutes until the additional ingredients are tender.

Ladle a couple of servings into a smaller pot and set
this aside to cool before refrigerating overnight for
day 4.

Continue to simmer the remaining soup in the big
pot. Take half of the saved portion of chicken wings
and warm it through gently in the oven or in a pan
before pulling the meat off the bone. Add the meat to
today's soup and simmer for a further 5–6 minutes.
Serve the soup topped with fresh aromatic herbs like
thyme leaves, or perhaps marjoram or tarragon.

Day 4

2 x 400ml (13.5fl oz) cans of coconut milk

2 tsp Caribbean curry powder

handful of chopped spring onions (scallions)

2 chillies of your choice, finely chopped

1 lime or lemon

On day 4, bring the pot of soup to the boil one
last time.

Add the coconut milk and curry powder along
with 200ml (scant 1 cup) water. Add the remaining
portion of leftover chicken wings and simmer for
15 minutes until the meat is piping hot.

Ladle the soup into bowls and top with finely
chopped spring onions (scallions) and chillies. Finish
with a squeeze of lime or lemon juice.

Note to reader

*Don't worry if you haven't got any leftover roast potatoes
(which is often the case at my house), just go with
whatever veg you do have at home or pick up some
extra potatoes from the greengrocer, market, or
supermarket if you like.*

Tea-brined spiced barbecue chicken

Serves 6
Prep time 20 minutes, plus brining time
Cook time 30–40 minutes

6 chicken thighs, skin on and bone in

6 chicken drumsticks, skin on and bone in

1 lemon, halved

For the brine

3 Earl Grey tea bags

peeled skin from 2 clementines

2 sprigs of thyme, leaves picked

2½ tsp sugar of your choice

1¾ tbsp table salt

1 litre (4⅓ cups) boiling water

For the seasoning paste

6 spring onions (scallions), roughly chopped

4 garlic cloves, roughly chopped

1½ tbsp rapeseed (canola) oil

2 tsp ground cumin

2 tsp paprika

1 tsp cayenne pepper

salt and freshly ground black pepper, to taste

For the final glaze

1 tbsp tamarind concentrate

1 tbsp molasses

1 tsp sugar of your choice

100ml (generous ⅓ cup) chicken stock

food processor
charcoal or gas barbecue (grill)

There's a lot of brining chat these days isn't there? To brine or not to brine, that is the question. I would say I'm firmly on the side of brine. It means you start to pack in the flavour early on and it really does bring a succulence to the meat. This recipe uses an Earl Grey tea brine, which holds the citrus flavour of bergamot at its heart. Combine that with the lemon zest in the barbecue spice rub, and it brings that extra bit of something special to a barbecue.

First, make your tea brine. Put the Earl Grey tea bags, clementine peel, thyme, sugar, and salt in a pot that is large enough to hold your chicken. Cover with the boiling water, stir a little to help dissolve the sugar and salt and allow to cool.

Take the two lemon halves and rub them all over the chicken. Now, put the chicken into the brine mixture, making sure it's covered by the liquid. Place in the fridge and leave for a minimum of 4 hours, or even better, overnight.

In the morning (or after 4 hours), blitz together all the ingredients for the seasoning paste in a food processor to make a thick paste.

Remove the chicken from the brine, pat it dry and add to a large bowl with the seasoning paste. Give the chicken a good rub all over with the paste, making sure it's completely coated. Leave to marinate in the fridge for at least 1 hour, ideally 3 hours or even a bit longer if you have time.

Heat the barbecue (grill) to a high heat. When it's hot, sear the chicken all over to give it a nice bit of colour, then reduce the heat if using a gas barbecue, or move over indirect heat for charcoal. Cook the chicken low and slow for about 40 minutes with the lid closed, turning occasionally, and brushing the meat with more of the spice paste as you go.

Meanwhile, combine all the ingredients for the final glaze together in a saucepan. Set over a medium heat and bubble until thickened.

Brush the glaze over the chicken for the final 10 minutes of cooking, turning the chicken over often and making sure the glaze covers every part. When the juices of the chicken run clear, the chicken is cooked. Brush one last time with the glaze, remove from the heat and rest for about 20 minutes.

Serve with Ducana (see page 33) or Spiced Roast Ground Provision (see page 164) and a simple salad with fresh herbs.

Hard-grilled fast midweek curry fish

Serves 2
Prep time 10 minutes, plus 30 minutes marinating
Cook time 20 minutes

This works with any kind of fish, but my favourites are most definitely at the oilier end of things. Something with a bit of body works best – a mackerel, a bass, a bream, even a piece of wild salmon. It's quick-quick fast-fast and loads of bang for your buck.

about 800g (1¾lb) whole fish such as 2 medium sea bass or bream, scaled and gutted (you can ask your fishmonger to do this for you)

150ml (⅔ cup) Green Seasoning (see page 110)

2 green bird's-eye chillies, finely chopped

10g (⅓oz) finely grated fresh ginger

grated zest of 2 limes

3 tsp Caribbean curry powder

2 tsp garam masala

cooking oil of your choice, for rubbing

about 100ml (generous ⅓ cup) fish or chicken stock

1 heaped tsp unsalted butter

salt and freshly ground black pepper

Wash the fish in very cold water, then pat dry with a piece of kitchen paper (paper towel). Transfer the fish to a chopping board and score the skin with a very sharp knife to ensure that your seasoning can penetrate the fish effectively. Put the fish into a wide bowl.

Pour most of the green seasoning over the fish (saving about 1 teaspoon for the sauce) and give it a good mix around so the fish is fully coated. Add the chillies, ginger, and lime zest, then rub the curry powder and garam masala all over, making sure it goes inside the cavity of the fish as well. Season to taste with salt and pepper, then cover the bowl with cling film (plastic wrap) and leave to marinate in the fridge for 30 minutes.

Preheat the grill (broiler) to its highest setting.

Line a grill tray with tin foil and rub with oil. Lay the marinated fish on top. Slip the tray into the preheated grill and hard-grill until the skin on the fish is popping and has a lovely deep golden colour, perhaps blackened and charred in places. Flip it over and do the same on the other side. (It should take about 8 minutes per side.)

Pour off the juices that have come from the fish into a saucepan, add the fish or chicken stock and the reserved teaspoon of the green seasoning. Bubble it all up, then whisk in the butter until melted and combined. Pour the sauce back over the fish and serve with a crisp green salad and a roti, or some Lemon & Garlic Dressed Callaloo (see page 125) and Coconut Rice (see page 67).

Saltfish salad

Serves 2
Prep time 15 minutes

In Antigua we call this a saltfish salad, in Trinidad it's a saltfish buljol – whatever you call it, I LOVE it. Fresh and zesty with herbal notes and just the right amount of spicy kick, this is a classic part of a Sunday morning Antiguan breakfast. Served with Johnny Cakes (see page 48), Lemon Salted Cucumbers (see page 127), sticky boiled eggs, souse, Sweet Potato Pudding (see page 177) and some dressed avocado, chop-up, and maybe even a bit of crispy bacon, it's Antiguan breakfast perfection!

500g (1lb 2oz) skinless and boneless saltfish such as ling, cod, or pollock

100g (3½oz) sweet green or yellow peppers, deseeded and grated

3–4 spring onions (scallions), thinly sliced

1 chilli (medium heat), thinly sliced

2 sprigs of thyme, leaves picked

2 sprigs oregano, leaves picked and finely chopped

20g (¾ oz) flat-leaf parsley, leaves picked and finely chopped

1 tbsp Green Seasoning (see page 110)

juice of 1 lemon

juice of 1 lime, plus extra to serve

3½ tbsp extra virgin rapeseed (canola) oil

generous pinch of ground black pepper

Mum's Lemon Salted Cucumbers (see page 127), to serve

1 avocado, to serve

First, rinse the saltfish thoroughly, then put it into a pot and cover with fresh cold water. Bring to the boil, then drain the water. Repeat this boiling process twice more using fresh water each time to get rid of the excess salt. Set the fish aside in a bowl to cool.

Once cooled, flake the fish gently with a fork until no large chunks remain.

In a large bowl, combine the grated peppers, spring onions (scallions), chilli, herbs, green seasoning, citrus juices, oil, and black pepper. Throw in the flaked fish and give everything a good, thorough mix up.

To serve, halve the avocado, remove the stone and skin and finely dice one half of the flesh. Add this to the lemon salted cucumbers and mix well.

Thinly slice the rest of the avocado and lay the slices onto serving plates. Top with the saltfish salad and serve with the lemon salted cucumbers and diced avocado. Finish with an extra squeeze of lime juice.

This breakfast salad goes wonderfully with a boiled egg, boiled for about 6 minutes until the centre is sticky.

Wadadli Kitchen spiced roast chicken with coconut gravy

Serves 4–6
Prep time 15 minutes
Cook time 1 hour 30 minutes

1 x 1.5–2kg (2¼–3lb 3oz) chicken (ideally free-range and organic)

1 yellow onion, halved

3 garlic cloves, peeled

1 sprig of thyme

For the Wadadli spice paste

1 heaped tsp ground turmeric

1 heaped tsp ground cumin

1 heaped tsp ground coriander

1 heaped tsp finely grated fresh ginger

80ml (⅓ cup) rapeseed (canola) oil

4 garlic cloves, peeled

1 large or 2 small spring onion(s) (scallions), roughly chopped

small handful of flat-leaf parsley

small handful of coriander (cilantro)

1–2 red or green bird's-eye chillies, to taste, roughly chopped

1 tsp sea salt

twist of freshly ground black pepper

For the coconut gravy

25g (scant 1oz) block of coconut cream

1 x 400ml (13.5fl oz) can of coconut milk

salt and freshly ground black pepper

food processor

This is a roast chicken, but not as you know it. The spice rub asserts itself to just the right degree, and the gravy is the stuff that (my) coconutty dreams are made of. I think it's a great way to bring changes to a roast, whilst still staying true to its heart. A recipe like this is where both sides of my British and Caribbean heart meet and embrace.

Preheat the oven to 130°C fan (150°C/300°F/Gas 2).

Put all the spice paste ingredients into a food processor and blitz together. Set aside.

Lay the chicken in a deep roasting tray and push both halves of the onion, the garlic cloves, and the sprig of thyme into the cavity. Pour the spiced paste all over the chicken, turning the bird around a couple of times in the paste to make sure it's well coated. Sprinkle with a good pinch of salt, cover the whole tray with tin foil and slip into the preheated oven for 1 hour.

Remove the tray from the oven and take off the tin foil. Using a big spoon, baste the chicken with all the lovely cooking juices, then pour off most of the juices into a saucepan.

Now to crisp up the spiced skin. Pop the tray back into the oven and turn the heat up to 200°C fan (220°C/425°F/Gas 7). After about 15–20 minutes, the skin should be crispy, but if it's not then just roast for 5–10 minutes more until it's right where you need it.

Meanwhile, add the coconut cream to the chicken juices in the saucepan and let it melt over a medium–low heat. Add the coconut milk, give it a stir and bring to a gentle simmer. If your chicken is ready, tip any remaining cooking juices in and reduce over a medium heat for around 7–10 minutes and hey presto – you have a coconut gravy! Season with salt and pepper to your taste. If it's a little thick, just add a splash of water and simmer to bring it together again until you are happy with the consistency.

Transfer the chicken to a serving platter and serve with crunchy golden roast potatoes – I often use WHITE sweet potatoes as a side – and all the other usual roast accompaniments like Yorkshire puddings, greens, carrots, peas, roast parsnips, or whatever takes your fancy!

Fish tea

Serves 6–8
Prep time 20 minutes
Cook time 45 minutes

Tea is what we call a light broth, so this is really a light but flavoursome and richly seasoned soup.

1 tbsp unsalted butter

2 tbsp extra virgin rapeseed (canola) oil

1 onion, thinly sliced

3 garlic cloves, thinly sliced

1 celery stick, finely diced

1 tsp coriander seeds

1 tsp whole allspice berries

1 tsp cumin seeds

½ tsp chilli flakes

1 red chilli, finely chopped

250g (9oz) pumpkin, peeled, deseeded, and cut into small cubes

1 carrot, peeled and finely diced

2 new potatoes, cut into quarters

2 eddoes (optional), peeled and finely diced

1 large plantain or green banana, sliced

1 litre (4⅓ cups) good quality fish stock

1 Scotch bonnet, left whole

small bunch of thyme

1 big bunch of spinach, shredded (optional)

6 red snapper fillets

salt and freshly ground black pepper

lemon wedges, to serve

Heat a large pot over a medium heat and add the butter and oil. Add the onion, garlic, and celery and sweat down until soft and translucent.

Add the spices, red chilli, and the rest of the vegetables and cook for around 10 minutes, stirring occasionally, until the veg takes on some colour.

Pour in the fish stock, season with salt and pepper, and chuck in the whole Scotch bonnet and thyme. Leave to gently bubble away for about 15–20 minutes until the veg is tender.

Scatter the shredded spinach into the pot, if using, then lay the fish on top. Cover with a lid and cook for 8–10 minutes until the fish is done.

Time to serve. Divide the fish between serving bowls and top with the vegetables and broth. Finish with a squeeze of lemon juice and an extra twist of black pepper.

Fry fish & escovitch pickle

Serves 4
Prep time 20 minutes
Cook time 10 minutes

This is one of the most pleasing ways to eat a piece of fried fish. Have it with one of the bread or dumpling recipes in the book and YES mama! Toe-curling happiness achieved.

250g (1¾ cups plus 2 tbsp) plain (all-purpose) flour

big pinch of ground paprika

big pinch of ground coriander

big pinch of ground cumin

big pinch of ground allspice

big pinch of salt

350g (12oz) fresh fish fillets (or around 2 whole scaled and gutted fish), such as snapper, sea bream, bass, or mullet

150ml (⅔ cup) milk of your choice

about 80ml (⅓ cup) neutral oil, such as rapeseed (canola) or sunflower oil, for frying

For the escovitch pickle

1 white onion or shallot

1 Scotch bonnet (or 2 if you like it truly hot hot)

½ carrot

½ red pepper, deseeded

½ green pepper, deseeded

250ml (1 cup plus 1 tbsp) white wine vinegar

1⅔ tbsp white sugar

1 tsp allspice berries

1 tsp juniper berries

1 tsp black peppercorns

First, prepare the pickle. Slice the onion, chilli, carrot, and peppers evenly and very thinly – I use a mandolin to make it easier, but a good sharp knife will do just as well, it just takes a little longer.

Add the vinegar, sugar, spices, and 3½ tablespoons of water to a saucepan and bring up to a simmer over a medium heat, stirring a little to dissolve the sugar. Remove from the heat and add the vegetables to the pan. Leave to cool and pickle while you prepare the fish for frying.

Mix together the flour, spices, and salt in a large bowl. Take the whole fish or the fillets and dip them first into the milk, then into the seasoned flour on both sides. Lay the fish on a board and chill in the fridge for around 20 minutes.

Remove the fish from the fridge, then heat about half of the oil in a heavy-based non-stick frying pan over a medium heat.

Slip the fish into the hot oil. If you're making this with whole fish, then fry one whole fish at a time. If you're using fillets, just fry two at a time.

Fry until the fish is golden all over – this will only take a few minutes on each side. Remove from the pan and transfer to a plate lined with kitchen paper (paper towels) to drain the excess oil. Repeat the frying process with the remaining fish and oil.

Pile the fried fish onto a serving plate, then spoon the pickle on top to serve.

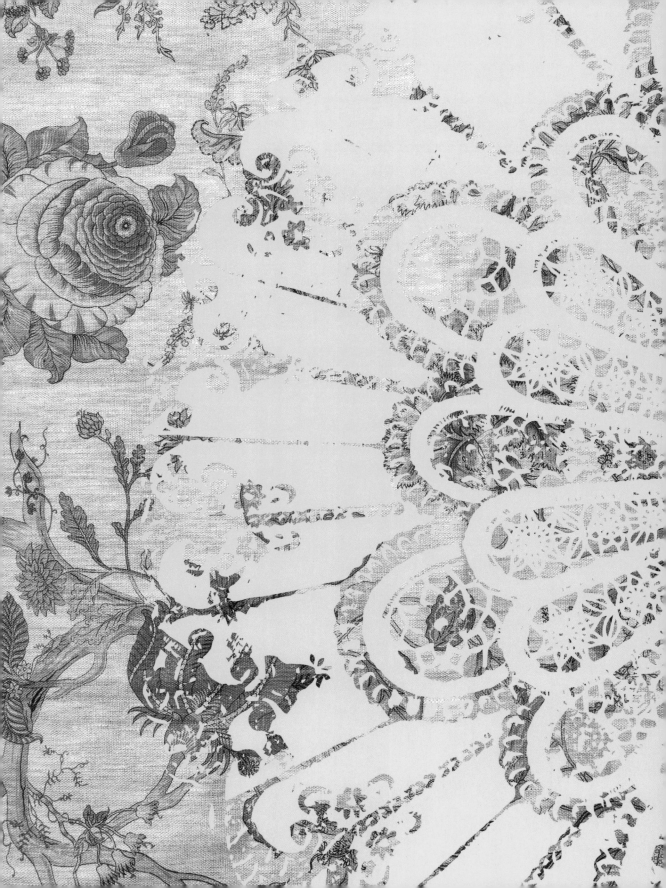

Weekend & celebration cooking

The weekend is a wonderful time if you love to be in the kitchen. Suddenly there is all this space and flow that can evade us during the hurried weeks. The same is true of high days and holidays. It's a time to experiment, play around with new ingredients and squeeze new flavours out of old dishes.

I know that for a cook who is less used to having big parties to cook for, or even a small party for an important event, the pressure can be a bit overwhelming. I find there are a few ways in which you can ease this pressure, and the main trick is to give yourself time. Don't try to do it all on one day. Make a good, comprehensive list a few days before the occasion. Shop at least one or two days before. Work out what the big jobs are and get them going the day before. Work out which smaller jobs you can tick off, get them done and leave them in the fridge or freezer.

Remember, it's supposed to be FUN! You are also meant to enjoy yourself. I often think that if you're new to big gathering cooking, it's a good idea to have ONE central focal point and then make a few simple, delicious things to surround it. As you gain confidence, this will evolve and you can go WILD, but my advice to start with is, please darlings, to pace yourselves. And don't forget cooks' treats. I am partial to a lovely glass of ice-cold Champagne with a splash of peach juice, or with a couple of black cherries soaked in Kirsch dropped in. Of course, it doesn't have to be alcoholic, but it should feel like a special thing just for you. The world is your oyster, have what you like – but if it's boozy have it slowly! You've still got the cooking to do!

Saturday 27th February

The ties that bind. Family, family, family, Neneh!

I couldn't really write this book without talking about cooking with Neneh. Neneh is my *other* other half really; in the kitchen and on the dance floor and for most of my adult life.

We've been through a LOT together... love, death, birth, joy, pain, failure, success, and always *always* cooking. Cooking is our first AND second language. It's our dance, it's our shorthand and our direct route back to each other when we haven't had the chance to look into each other's eyes in too long a while, which frankly happens way too often these days.

We were so young when we met, still babies really (although we felt fully grown), and I had never known someone who completely understood so many things about me that I hadn't even worked out myself yet. We brought our children up together and now WE are the aunties and the godmothers and Neneh is a grandmother. It feels like just the other day we were those hopeful, open-hearted teenage girls, making up dance routines, cooking chicken, making hot toddies, soaking up all and any music, listening to Richard Pryor records, singing and dancing on stage or on the street and playing tunes in the clubs of beautiful, filthy, glorious old Soho (God, I miss that place!). We taught each other how to be ourselves.

So, cooking for us is a beautiful thing; it's our church and our sacred ritual. These days, because we're both so intensely busy, it mostly happens at carnival for an endless stream of hungry, seemingly hugely tall (or are we shrinking?) shining, wonderful young men and women on our favourite weekend of the year.

It used to be us out there on those streets, and almost without blinking we have become the Mamas. We had a conversation recently during which we realized that we are turning into the women we used to read about in books by Ntozake Shange, Alice Walker, Toni Morrison, Rebecca Wells, Buchi Emecheta. Those books and those authors shone a light for us through the dark tunnel of youthful self-discovery, and we will be eternally grateful.

We are the ladies with the bubbly pear cider at the party in the park with a nice chair to sit on. How this has happened is beyond my comprehension, but it appears to be true. So whether it's for a birthday, Christmas, Thanksgiving, an anniversary, or even a couple of years ago for her new album launch party, we do what we do.

One of us will start a pot, the other one will come in and finish it. One of us will season the chicken, the other one will get the barbecue going and get it on the grill. Then we take turns to come in and turn the meat, brushing it with a shining, smoky-hot, sweet glaze that we have made with our heads close together, speaking our sweet sister language.

One of us will soak the black beans and simmer them until they're tender, swirling them with thyme, garlic, onions, marjoram, cardamom, coriander and cumin seeds and such like, then the other will finish them off in the pot, adjusting the seasoning, adding little bits of loveliness until it's balanced. A bit of soy sauce there, a spoonful of tamarind here, a scattering of spring onions (scallions), a drop or two of molasses, a handful of fresh herbs to bring it all together.

Often, we're combining the Caribbean traditions with Southern American soul food pathways, and actually a little touch of Sweden (another part of Neneh's heritage) and a little bit of Britain from me too. It's fascinating how much it all mirrors each other. It's like a lifelong ongoing conversation that lives so deep within us it is medicine. It reminds me that in different parts of the world, Black people, we of the African diaspora, carry our ancestors in our pots and on our tables and in our instinct in the kitchen.

When I think of celebration cooking, I think of Neneh. Of all the years of US. In the kitchen it's just us in our flowing, unspoken rhythm. It's the time that we make for each other, and I love it and of course her. She showed me how to find my freedom, my fire, and my joy. She remains the most extraordinary of women. Neneh, I love you always and forever. I am so proud of you, sis, so proud of both of us. Thank you x.

The first of the two recipes that follow is a new one in the family celebratory arsenal. I came up with it a few Christmases ago with Tyson, Neneh's middle daughter. It's completely delicious and has now become a staple for us on Christmas morning, with a glass of something cold, bubbly, and refreshing. The second of these recipes is a dish which our children (and all the other nieces, nephews, and godchildren) have grown up on, and they all beg for it on Saturdays, Sundays, birthdays, carnival, and all of the aforementioned high days and holidays.

ON THE MENU TODAY

BERRY & CHILLI SHRUB CURED SALMON

HONEY BAKED CHICKEN

GOLDEN TURMERIC MAYONNAISE

RUM PUNCH

Berry & chilli shrub cured salmon

Serves 10
Prep time 10 minutes, plus marinating time

Right so... anatomy of a recipe here we go. My niece Tyson and I came up with this one Christmas. She'd been working with the brilliant Missy, who is one half of the brains and passion alongside Gabriel Pryce at the excellent Rita's Dining in one of their incarnations. Tyson had been experimenting with an old fashioned way of pickling fruit used in a cocktail called a shrub. We took the shrub and played around with it, adding chilli and Caribbean ingredients we thought could work well on our Christmas salmon. Hey presto, we discovered the chilli shrub cure and my my, isn't she lovely!

1kg (2¼lb) frozen summer fruits, defrosted, plus extra to garnish (optional)

250g (1¼ cups) white sugar

250g (1¾ cups) rock salt

1 red chilli, finely chopped

grated zest of 1 orange, plus extra to garnish (optional)

150ml (⅔ cup) mezcal

200ml (scant 1 cup) cider vinegar

2 tbsp Green Seasoning (see page 110)

1kg (2¼lb) side of salmon (the freshest and best quality you can get)

To make the cure, mix the defrosted berries, sugar, salt, chilli, orange zest, mezcal, vinegar, and green seasoning together in a large bowl.

Place the salmon in a deep, long tray and pour over the cure. Make sure the cure completely covers the salmon from top to bottom. Cover with cling film (plastic wrap) and leave in the fridge for at least 1 day.

Remove the salmon from the cure and pat dry. Slice thinly and enjoy as a light lunch with warm coco bread and a fresh, crisp salad, or garnish with extra berries and orange zest and serve as part of a large celebration meal.

Honey baked chicken

Serves 4-6
Prep time 20 minutes, plus marinating time
Cook time 1 hour 20 minutes

Gosh, this recipe is home really. My dear friend Neneh and I have worked on this dish for many years. Each year at carnival it gets a new interpretation with something different to offer. This chicken is what all the kids want when they're happy, sad, or just plain hungry. It's comfort and excitement all at once.

12 chicken thighs and drumsticks, skin on and bone in

150g (½ cup) clear honey

250ml (1 cup plus 1 tbsp) chicken stock

For the marinade

2 onions, finely chopped

6 garlic cloves, crushed

20g (¾oz) fresh ginger, grated

15g (½oz) flat-leaf parsley, finely chopped

15g (½oz) coriander (cilantro), finely chopped

10g sprigs of thyme, leaves picked and finely chopped

2 Scotch bonnet chillies, finely chopped

juice of 2 limes

juice of 2 lemons

juice of 2 oranges

4 tbsp soy sauce or tamari

1 tsp ground nutmeg

1 tbsp English mustard or mustard of your choice

1 tsp ground allspice

5 tbsp dark rum

2 tbsp olive oil

salt and freshly ground black pepper, to taste

Place all the marinade ingredients in a large bowl and mix well. Add the chicken pieces to the bowl and mix with your hands to coat each piece in the marinade. Cover the bowl with cling film (plastic wrap) and leave to marinate in the fridge for at least 1 hour, or preferably overnight.

Preheat the oven to 160°C fan (180°C/350°F/Gas 4).

Remove the chicken pieces from the bowl of marinade and transfer them to a roasting tray, skin-side up. Reserve the bowl of leftover marinade and set aside in the fridge. Bake the chicken in the middle of the preheated oven for 50–60 minutes, checking the chicken after 15–20 minutes, basting with the juices and turning the pieces over. You can also flip the tray around to make sure it's all cooking evenly.

When the chicken pieces are golden and the juices are running clear, they're cooked. Drizzle the honey all over the chicken and slip the tray back into the oven for a further 10 minutes, or until sticky and caramelized.

Meanwhile, add the reserved marinade to a pan with the chicken stock and any juices from the chicken tray. Bring to the boil and bubble until reduced and thickened to serve with the chicken.

Golden turmeric mayonnaise

Serves 6
Prep time 10 minutes

Turmeric is one of my favourite spices. Smoky and fragrant, it's a wonderful addition to this mayonnaise. Dip everything and anything in it.

1 whole egg

1 egg yolk

400ml (1¾ cups) cold pressed extra virgin rapeseed (canola) oil or any neutral oil

1 tsp English mustard

1¾ tsp ground turmeric

juice of 1 lemon

2 fat garlic cloves, peeled (swap these for roasted garlic cloves for a sweeter flavour if you prefer)

pinch of freshly ground black pepper

big fat pinch of sea salt – I like Maldon best

hand-held blender

Throw all the ingredients into a deep jug or jar. Using a hand-held blender, simply blitz until it all comes together and emulsifies into a mayonnaise-like texture.

Taste and adjust the seasoning to your liking; you may want to add another pinch of salt.

Rum punch

There is, of course, many a rum punch recipe. I often find them overly sweet, so we've come up with our own family version, which I think has just the right balance of rum, juices, and coconut – and still keeps the BOOM!!

200ml (scant 1 cup) aged gold rum

150ml (⅔ cup) gold rum

300ml (1¼ cups) coconut milk

400ml (1¾ cups) coconut water

300ml (1¼ cups) guava juice

200ml (scant 1 cup) orange and mango juice

1 tsp grenadine

1 tsp orange bitters

2 tbsp agave syrup

4 tsp ginger syrup (from a jar of preserved stem ginger in syrup)

3 handfuls of ice

extra ice, to serve

fresh limes, to serve

blender

Add all the ingredients to a blender and blitz them up. Pour the punch into glasses over extra ice to serve, and finish with an extra squeeze of fresh lime juice.

If you prefer it sweeter, you can add more agave syrup or another sweetener of your choice.

Barbecue shrimp with chilli spiked butter

Serves 2–4
Prep time 20 minutes
Cook time 8 minutes

Things I dream about number 375... being in Antigua with a barbecue on and a tray of achingly fresh seafood to burnish on the grill. As soon as I smell that char, I'm transported back to high days and holidays in Antigua, and the first time I made these golden shrimp slathered in chilli butter. It's a super speedy, super delicious dish which looks beautiful on a huge platter.

1kg (2¼lb) shell-on king prawns (jumbo shrimp), deveined

4 tbsp Green Seasoning (see page 110)

2 limes or lemons, halved

For the butter

2 long red chillies, roughly chopped

1 tsp garlic purée

1 tsp runny honey

1 tsp Green Seasoning (see page 110)

1 spring onion (scallion), roughly chopped

big pinch of sea salt flakes, plus extra to serve

couple of twists of black pepper

125g (1 stick plus 1 tbsp) unsalted butter, softened

barbecue (grill)

blender

Combine the prawns with the green seasoning in a bowl and give them a good mix up so that all the prawns are well coated. Leave to marinate for 1 hour. It's very important that you do NOT add any lime or lemon juice at this point as the acid would start to change the texture of the seafood.

Fire up your barbecue (grill).

Add all the chilli butter ingredients, apart from the butter, to a blender and blitz to a smooth paste. Stir the spice paste into the softened butter in a bowl until thoroughly mixed. Transfer the butter to a ramekin or roll it into a sausage shape inside a piece of cling film (plastic wrap) and twist the ends to seal. Refrigerate until needed.

When your barbecue is smouldering hot, place your marinated prawns on the grill. Cook for about 2–3 minutes on each side until they are pink, plump, and juicy. Drop pieces of chilli butter over the prawns as they cook and allow them to melt in.

When the prawns are nearly ready, add the lemon or lime halves to the grill and let them char, flesh-side down.

Remove the prawns from the grill and serve immediately with a squeeze of charred lime or lemon juice, extra sea salt flakes and a final knob of that spiked chilli butter.

Note to reader
If a barbecue isn't available, you can cook the prawns in the same way on a sizzling hot, heavy-based pan with a drizzle of oil.

Rum & ginger braised pork ribs

Serves 6–8
Prep time 15 minutes
Cook time 3½–4½ hours

An ice-cold, 10-year-aged English Harbour Antiguan rum with ginger ale over ice. This is the way I was introduced to rum, and it's still my favourite way to drink it. This recipe is my go-to rum drink in a cooking pot. The sugars from the ginger ale and the rum work on the ribs during the slow-cook, until they are melting and unctuous.

neutral oil, such as rapeseed (canola) or sunflower oil, for frying

4kg (8¾lb) pork ribs

200g (7oz) sliced onion

5 garlic cloves, grated

1 tsp cumin seeds

15g (½oz) grated fresh ginger

100g (3½oz) chopped tomatillo (if available)

100g (3½oz) tomatoes, grated

100g (3½oz) tomatoes, chopped

250ml (1 cup plus 1 tbsp) dark or golden rum

1 litre (4⅓ cups) chicken stock

1 litre (4⅓ cups) ginger ale

200g (1¾ sticks) unsalted butter

In a hot frying pan, sear the ribs on each side in a little oil until they take on a deep golden colour. Remove from pan and leave to one side.

Find a large, lidded, braising pan that's wide enough for the whole ribs to fit in. Set the pan over a medium–low heat with a splash of oil. Add the onion and garlic and cook for about 10 minutes until softened.

Add the cumin seeds and ginger and sauté for a further 5 minutes. Add the tomatillos (if using) and grated and chopped tomatoes and sauté for another 5 minutes.

Finally, add the seared ribs, rum, chicken stock, and ginger ale. Cover the pan with the lid and leave over a low heat to braise gently for 3–4 hours until the ribs are meltingly tender.

Remove the ribs from the pot and place on a large plate or dish to one side. Turn the heat up under the cooking liquid. When it's bubbling vigorously, whisk in the butter until melted, then pour the sauce back over the ribs and serve.

Patties

Makes 8–10
Prep time 20 minutes, plus 1 hour
20 minutes chill time
Cook time 20–25 minutes

Immediately connected to Jamaica for so many, the patty is, of course, something you will find all over the Caribbean. The pastry in a *Jamaican* patty, though, is flaky, yellow-golden, and delicious. The origins of the recipe are interesting, because it is in fact a version of the Cornish pasty, which was brought to Caribbean shores by colonizers/enslavers, and which then became intertwined with the cooking of African and Indian peoples in the Caribbean. Fill them with whatever you want, I am split between a curry goat one or a saltfish filling, and then of course there's the curried shrimp and curried chana... what's your favourite?

Flip back to the Curries in the Caribbean section of this book (see pages 72–103) and pick one.

525g (scant 4 cups) plain (all-purpose) flour, plus extra for dusting

250g (2 sticks) cold unsalted butter, diced

1 tsp Caribbean curry powder

1 tsp ground turmeric

1½ tsp fine salt

1 x curry of your choice for the filling (see pages 72–103)

1–2 eggs, beaten, for brushing

Put the flour and butter in a large bowl and rub together to form a rough crumb. It's okay to have some more lumpy bits of butter left over, as this will help the pastry turn out more flaky. Add 180ml (¾ cup) of cold water and mix to bring the dough together, taking care not to overwork it. Cover the bowl of dough with cling film (plastic wrap) and place in the fridge to rest and chill for 1 hour.

Tip the dough out onto a lightly floured work surface and use a rolling pin to roll it out in one direction to make a rough rectangle shape, with one of the shorter edges closest to you. You want it to be around the thickness of a 50p coin (roughly 2–3mm/⅛in). The dough should have a marbled look from the pieces of chilled butter.

Fold the top third of the dough into the centre, then the bottom third over that. Roll the pastry out again to the same thickness and shape. Repeat the same folding process, then wrap the dough in cling film and chill for a further 20 minutes in the fridge.

Preheat the oven to 180°C fan (200°C/400°F/Gas 6).

Remove the dough from the fridge and roll it out once more on a lightly floured work surface to the thickness of a 50p coin (roughly 2–3mm/⅛in).

Using a bowl, saucer, or cookie cutter, cut out 8–10 circles of pastry, around 15cm (6in) in size. Put a tablespoon of your chosen filling into the middle of each pastry circle. Brush the edges of the pastry lightly with beaten egg, then fold half the pastry over the top to enclose the filling and make semi-circle shapes. Crimp the edges of the pastry together using a fork.

Transfer the patties to a baking sheet lined with baking parchment, evenly spaced apart. Brush them all with beaten egg, then bake the patties in the preheated oven for 20–25 minutes until the pastry is flaky and golden.

Leave to cool slightly or fully before serving.

Shrimp fritters

Makes 12
Prep time 15 minutes
Cook time 15 minutes

Crisp on the outside and fluffy on the inside, I suggest you make a huge pile of these and serve them with your favourite hot sauce and an ice-cold beer! Just make sure your batter doesn't get too wet, if you're worried just add a little more flour.

100g (¾ cup) plain (all-purpose) flour

1 tsp baking powder

½ tsp cayenne pepper

½ tsp paprika

½ tsp ground allspice

3 eggs

2 tbsp cold sparkling water

200g (7oz) king prawns (jumbo shrimp), peeled, deveined, and very finely chopped

3 spring onions (scallions), finely chopped

grated zest of 1 lemon

salt and freshly ground black pepper

750ml (3¼ cups) neutral oil, such as rapeseed (canola) or sunflower oil, for deep-frying

Stir together the flour and spices in a large bowl. Crack in the eggs and pour in the cold sparkling water. Whisk it up until you have a smooth, thick batter.

Stir in the prawns, spring onions (scallions), lemon zest, and salt and pepper to taste.

Heat the oil in a deep-fat fryer or heavy-based saucepan to 170°C (340°F). To test whether the oil is hot enough, drop in a cube of white bread. If it bubbles straight away and goes golden, then the oil is ready for frying.

Carefully slip in tablespoons of the fritter mixture, cooking in batches of 4 at a time for about 5 minutes. When the fritters are crisp and golden-brown, remove from the oil with a slotted spoon and drain the excess oil on a plate lined with kitchen paper (paper towels). Tear one open to make sure the prawns are pink/white and cooked all the way through – this is the chef's treat!

Repeat the frying process with the remaining batter and serve straight away.

Slow-cooked lamb 3 ways

Lamb cassareep

Serves 6
Prep time 20 minutes, plus marination time
Cook time 4 hours

When I was a child, I lived in Cyprus for a few years. This experience has indelibly left its mark on my cooking brain, and influenced the textures and flavours that I reach for at times. Slow-cooked, succulent aromatic lamb with all its little crispy bits of fat is definitely one of those things. This recipe is both my past and present worlds colliding – it's those Greek Cypriot textures and Antiguan seasonings married together.

2kg (4½lb) leg of lamb

1 medium cup of freshly brewed coffee left to cool slightly (about 100–120ml/generous ⅓–½ cup)

200ml Green Seasoning (see page 110)

2 red chillies, finely chopped

2 tsp coriander seeds, roughly crushed

2 good pinches of sea salt

3 tbsp cassareep, or use molasses or treacle

1 x 400g (14oz) can of pitted prunes in their own juice

1 medium glass of red wine (175ml/¾ cup)

500ml (generous 2 cups) lamb or beef stock

hand-held blender or food processor

Score the skin of the lamb so that when you season it the herbs and spices can really get involved. Place the lamb in a large roasting tray. Pour over the coffee, then give the lamb a good old rub with the green seasoning, chillies, coriander seeds, salt, and cassareep – don't be shy, you want to make sure you are getting all the flavourings into every crack and crevice. Leave to marinate in the fridge for at least 3–4 hours, or ideally overnight.

Preheat the oven to 160°C fan (180°C/350°F/Gas 4).

Cover the tray of lamb with tin foil and slip into the preheated oven to slowly roast for around 3 hours.

After 3 hours, pour the roasting juices from the lamb into a saucepan and return the lamb to the oven. Add the prunes and their juice to the saucepan, along with the red wine and stock. Let this bubble up and reduce for about 10 minutes over a medium–high heat, then blitz until smooth with a hand-held blender or in a food processor.

Remove the lamb from the oven and pour the blended prune sauce over. Turn the heat up to 200°C fan (220°C/425°F/Gas 7) and slip the lamb back into the oven for a further 1 hour, or until it's tender and almost falling off the bone. Serve.

Slow-cooked spiced poached lamb

Serves 8–10
Prep time 15 minutes
Cook time 7 hours

This next lamb recipe is inspired by a trip I made to Morocco. I had the absolute honour of being invited into the extraordinary kitchen of the legendary and truly exceptional restaurant in Marrakesh called Al Fassia. The whole place is run and fully staffed by the most startlingly inspiring, talented, powerful women, who truly took my breath away. What a place, what a vibe, what stunning food! They taught me a technique to cook lamb that delivers the most heavenly results. I have taken the liberty of using their technique and marrying it with the flavours from the Caribbean that my heart yearns for.

1½ tsp ground turmeric

1 tsp paprika

1 tsp cayenne pepper

6 star anise

2 whole cloves

2 cinnamon sticks

3 bay leaves

20g (¾oz) grated fresh ginger

35g (1¼oz) finely chopped garlic

1 good fat pinch of salt

2kg (4½lb) lamb shoulder

3 red onions, finely diced

80g (generous ⅓ cup) melted unsalted butter

80ml (generous ⅓ cup) olive oil

Gently warm 2.5 litres (10½ cups) of water in a very large, deep saucepan. Add all the dried and whole spices, the bay leaves, ginger, garlic, and salt and bring to a gentle simmer. Slip the lamb shoulder into the pot. Pop in half of the chopped onions and cover the pan with a lid.

Continue to simmer gently over a low heat for 5–6 hours, until the meat is so soft that it's falling off the bone. Keep an eye on the liquid level in the pot as the lamb poaches, adding a little more water if it has reduced by more than half. (It's important to keep the water level up or the lamb will stick to the bottom of the pan, and you'll have no gorgeous sauce at the end.)

Preheat the oven to 180°C fan (200°C/400°F/Gas 6).

Remove the lamb from the poaching liquid (reserving the liquid to make a sauce) and transfer to a large roasting tray. Mix the melted butter and oil together and baste the lamb with this mixture. Slip the tray into the preheated oven and roast for about 30–40 minutes, basting every 10 minutes or so, until the lamb becomes crisp on the outside.

Meanwhile, remove 1.5 litres (6¼ cups) of the poaching liquid and transfer to a wide pan. You can discard any remaining poaching liquid or keep it to use in another dish (such as the Tamarind Torta Ahogada, see overleaf). Add the remaining onion to the wide pan and let the mixture bubble and reduce over a medium heat for about 30 minutes, until it has thickened slightly and become a lovely sauce.

Remove the lamb from the oven and transfer it to a platter. Pour over the sauce and serve. You don't really need to carve it as it's so soft, just spoon it up and pile it onto plates.

Tamarind torta ahogada

Serves 4
Prep time 15 minutes
Cook time 35 minutes

any leftover sauce from Slow-Cooked Spiced Poached Lamb (see page 229)

enough beef or lamb stock to make the total quantity of liquid up to 2 litres (8½ cups)

90g (3oz) wet tamarind, or use 2 tsp tamarind paste

3 tbsp passata (strained tomato sauce)

1 tbsp Green Seasoning (see page 110)

leftover roast lamb (at least 1 small handful per sandwich) from Slow-Cooked Spiced Poached Lamb (see page 229)

3 tbsp hot sauce of your choice, plus extra to serve

4 large brioche buns (I have used sourdough brioche because it is a bit more robust but standard will suffice)

For the radish pickle

150ml (⅔ cup) white wine vinegar

2 tsp white sugar

pinch of coriander seeds

pinch of black peppercorns

2 garlic cloves, peeled and smashed

1 bay leaf

1 bunch of radishes, topped and tailed and thinly sliced

very thinly sliced red or white onion, cucumber or anything else you want to grab to pickle (optional)

What a way with leftovers! I discovered the glory that is torta ahogada relatively recently and have since been seduced by its spell. The dish comes from Guadalajara in Mexico, and the name means quite literally drowned sandwich. I've come up with this torta ahogada, dripping in tamarind gravy, as a way of getting the most out of the end of your slow-cooked lamb. This can also, of course, be made with any meat or perhaps charred vegetables soaked in gravy – the possibilities are dreamy.

Take the leftover sauce from your lamb and combine it with half of your measured quantity of stock. Transfer to a saucepan and add the tamarind (whichever you are using). Bubble it all up together vigorously over a high heat for about 10 minutes.

Add the passata and green seasoning and bubble for another few minutes. Add the leftover meat, hot sauce, and the rest of the stock and simmer for about 8–10 more minutes to bring it all together.

Preheat the oven to 150°C fan (170°C/340°F/Gas 4).

Meanwhile, to make the pickle, add the vinegar, sugar, coriander seeds, peppercorns, garlic, and bay leaf to a small–medium saucepan. Simmer gently over a low heat for about 4–5 minutes until the sugar has dissolved. Remove from the heat and let cool slightly. Add the radishes and any other bits you want to pickle to a heatproof bowl, then pour the pickling liquid over and leave to pickle while you finish making the sandwiches.

Split the brioche buns in half and lay them open on a roasting tray with a lip at the sides. Take the tray to the meat pan and dip the inside of both the top and bottom of each bun into the sauce. Lay them back on the tray. Using a pair of tongs, fill each bun with the meat and sauce mixture. Add a few pickles to each bun, then put the top on each sandwich. Using a ladle, cover the buns with the rest of the saucy meat mixture (this is the drowned bit). Cover the tray with foil and slip into the preheated oven for about 10 minutes, then remove the foil and slip back into the oven for a final 5 minutes.

Remove from the oven and serve the sandwiches topped with an extra swirl of hot sauce and more pickles, if you wish.

WEEKEND

PIG TAIL. R
Bull FOOT,
SEASON RIC
LOBSTER

SS. PORK

UNGIE & CONCH

FRY FISH

Hominy corn, black beans, & crispy okra

Serves 4
Prep time 10 minutes
Cook time 25 minutes

Hominy corn is widely available in Antiguan supermarkets, and I have fallen in love with the nutty fullness of its flavour. I am usually all for swapping things out and working with what you can get, but with this I really want you to try to get your hands on hominy! There is not really anything else like it, so you'll be glad you went to the trouble. This recipe is a hit with my vegan dinner guests.

splash of rapeseed (canola) oil, for frying

1 large onion, thinly sliced

4 garlic cloves, grated

1 bird's-eye chilli, finely chopped

1 cinnamon stick

½ tsp ground green cardamom

½ tsp ground turmeric

1 x 425g (14oz) can of black beans, drained

1 x can of hominy corn (about 220g/8oz)

150ml (⅔ cup) coconut milk

100ml (generous ⅓ cup) vegetable stock

salt and freshly ground black pepper

For the crispy okra

100g (¾ cup) plain (all-purpose) flour

1 tbsp ground turmeric

100ml (generous ⅓ cup) cold sparkling water

160g (5½oz) okra

about 300ml (1¼ cups) neutral oil, such as rapeseed (canola) or sunflower oil, for frying

Add a splash of oil to a large saucepan and fry the onions over a medium heat for 5 minutes until softened. Add the garlic, chilli, and spices and stir to combine.

Add the black beans and hominy corn and give the pan a good stir to make sure it's all properly combined. Add the coconut milk, vegetable stock, and salt and pepper to taste. Turn up the heat and let the mixture bubble up vigorously for about 15 minutes until the liquid has reduced by about half – you want the texture to be more like a thick stew than a soup.

Meanwhile, make the batter by mixing the flour, turmeric, and sparkling water together in a large bowl. Season the batter with salt and pepper to taste. Cut the okra in half lengthwise.

Heat the oil in a deep-fat fryer or a heavy-based saucepan to 170°C (340°F). One by one, dunk the pieces of okra into the batter and slip them into the hot oil. Gently deep-fry until crisp and golden. Remove from the oil with a slotted spoon and place on a plate lined with kitchen paper (paper towels) to drain any excess oil.

Serve the stew in bowls topped with the crispy okra.

Confit chilli, orange & lemon salmon

Serves 6–8
Prep time 30 minutes, plus curing time
Cook time 30–35 minutes

1kg (2¼lb) side of salmon (the best quality and freshest you can get)

For the citrus zest mix

grated zest of 2 lemons

grated zest of 1 large orange

20g (¾oz) red chilli, finely chopped

For the cure

100g (¾ cup) coarse sea salt

20g (¾oz) citrus zest mix (see above)

6½ tbsp caster (superfine) sugar

For the citrus coconut vinaigrette

squeezed juice of 2 lemons

squeezed juice of 1 orange

90ml (⅓ cup) olive oil

2¼ tsp ground turmeric

90ml (⅓ cup) coconut milk

pinch of salt

pinch of black pepper

2½ tsp caster (superfine) sugar

For the confit

rind peeled from 1 lemon

rind peeled from 1 orange

20g (¾oz) red chilli, roughly chopped

8 garlic cloves, bashed

1 fresh bay leaf

700ml (scant 3 cups) olive oil

To garnish

handful of flat-leaf parsley

1 red chilli, chopped

leftover citrus zest mix (see above)

The lemons in Antigua look somewhere between a lemon and a lime. When I'm cooking there, I use them most every day. They are sweet and bright and I use the zest in all sorts of cures, confits, and marinades. For this recipe, I've also added some orange to broaden the citrus impact on the final plate. Lovely for any time of day, this salmon dish is elegant, subtle, and gentle.

Combine all the ingredients for the citrus zest mix in a bowl and set aside.

Add all the ingredients for the cure to a bowl and mix well. Lay the fish on a large sheet of cling film (plastic wrap) in a large dish. Liberally coat the salmon on all sides in the cure, then wrap in the cling film. Refrigerate for 1 hour 30 minutes.

Preheat the oven to 90°C (195°F).

Combine all the ingredients for the vinaigrette in a small bowl and put to one side.

Remove the salmon from the cure, rinse it off and pat dry. Transfer the salmon to a large ovenproof dish, then add all the confit ingredients, pouring in the oil last. Slip into the preheated oven for 30–35 minutes.

When the time is up, remove the dish from the oven and allow the salmon to sit in the warm oil for a further 5 minutes, or if you prefer the fish a little more done, let it sit for another 10 minutes.

Carefully remove the fish from the oil with a spatula and leave to cool before gently peeling the skin off the back of the fillet.

Place the fish in the middle of a large serving plate or platter. Spoon over the vinaigrette and pile the flat-leaf parsley, chilli, and remaining citrus zest mix on top to garnish.

Sweetcorn pudding

Serves 4
Prep time 10 minutes
Cook time 1 hour

The first time I ever encountered this dish was probably about 20 years ago at a party in West London. The brilliantly talented American chef Ashbell McElveen was cooking a vast universe of delicious dishes for his then new London restaurant. I was with my darling friend Neneh Cherry and her brother Eagle-Eye, and none of us had ever tasted anything like it. Instant enchantment. We subsequently discovered it's an American Southern soul food classic (sweetcorn pudding with fried chicken anyone? Yes, yes, Lord!). Ashbell was kind enough to give us his recipe on the night. It was love at first bite, creamy, soothing and delectable, it went straight into the family repertoire!

We make this for every Christmas, birthday, barbecue, summer picnic... any excuse basically. And nearly every time, I remember that first glorious time. Thank you, Ashbell.

300ml (1⅓ cups) double (heavy) cream

3 eggs

6⅓ tbsp unsalted butter, melted

4 tsp caster (granulated) sugar

good pinch of sea salt

340g (12oz) drained canned sweetcorn

handful of flat-leaf parsley

3 fat garlic cloves, chopped

food processor

deep, ovenproof casserole dish (about 1.5–2 litre/2¾–3½ pint capacity)

Preheat the oven to 160°C fan (180°C/350°F/Gas 4).

Blitz the cream, eggs, melted butter, sugar, and salt in a food processor until just evenly combined.

Throw in 3 tablespoons of the sweetcorn, the parsley, and garlic and give it one more blitz to thoroughly combine.

Tip the remaining sweetcorn into the ovenproof casserole dish, then pour the cream mixture over. Give it a little stir to combine. Carefully slip the casserole dish into the preheated oven and bake for about 1 hour, or until the pudding is lightly set with a very gentle wobble.

Serve with anything you like. Chicken of any kind is a favourite pairing for us – why not try it with Honey Baked Chicken (see page 213).

Cheese, leek, & smoked chilli rarebit B&B pudding

Bread & butter pudding? Yes! Cheese, YES. Hot, gooey, sticky loveliness, YES! This is all that and more, plus it's a great way to use up leftover bits of cheese and day-old bread. I made this for my make-up artist, the amazing Kellie Licorish, and she was instantly in love. We even had it the next morning, sliced and fried with crispy bacon. (I know, I know, she's banging on about bacon again... I just like bacon, okay?)

Serves 3–4
Prep time 40 minutes
Cook time 40 minutes

For the caramelized leeks

2 tsp unsalted butter

1 leek, thinly sliced

½ large onion, thinly sliced

salt and freshly ground black pepper

For the spring onion and garlic oil

2 spring onions (scallions)

4 garlic cloves, peeled

150ml (⅔ cup) rapeseed (canola) oil

For the bread & butter pudding

2 eggs

350ml (1½ cups) double (heavy) cream

80g (3oz) Parmesan, grated

80g (3oz) Gruyère, grated

120g (4½oz) mature (aged) Cheddar, grated

220g (8oz) caramelized leeks

2 tbsp spring onion and garlic oil

1 tsp English mustard or mustard of your choice

4 tbsp unsalted butter

280g (10oz) slightly stale sliced sourdough bread (about 8 medium slices)

salt and freshly ground black pepper

For the chipotle rarebit

1 tbsp chipotle paste (chipotle chilli powder)

2 egg yolks

1 tsp English mustard or mustard of your choice

160g (5½oz) mature (aged) Cheddar

a good glug of Worcestershire sauce

100ml (generous ⅓ cup) stout (I used Guinness, but any dark, rich ale works)

salt and freshly ground black pepper

food processor

First, make the caramelized leeks. Melt the butter over a low heat in a medium saucepan. Add the sliced leek and onion with a little salt and pepper and cook down slowly for about 30–40 minutes, stirring occasionally, until the leeks are dark and sticky.

Preheat the oven to 170°C fan (190°C/375°F/Gas 5).

To make a quick spring onion and garlic oil, simply blitz the spring onions (scallions) and garlic in a food processor with a little oil. (Note, this recipe makes more spring onion and garlic oil than you need, but leftovers will keep well in a jar in the fridge for up to 3–4 weeks).

For the bread and butter pudding, whisk together the eggs, cream, and grated cheeses in a large bowl. Stir through a quarter of the caramelized leeks, along with the spring onion and garlic oil and mustard. Season with salt and pepper, give it a good mix up and set to one side.

Butter both sides of your sourdough bread slices. Layer up the sliced buttered bread in a deep baking dish with spoonfuls of the remaining caramelized leeks and a good amount of salt and pepper between each layer.

Next, slowly pour three-quarters of the cream and cheese mixture over the layered bread. Give the dish a little shake back and forth to let the mixture really get into all the gaps. Leave the liquid to soak in for 5–10 minutes, then press down the top to really squish it all together and pour the remaining cheesy cream over.

Slip into the preheated oven and bake for 30–40 minutes, or until the pudding is set with a golden-brown crust. Remove from the oven and allow to cool for 10–20 minutes.

Once slightly cooled, place a sheet of baking parchment on top of the bread and butter pudding, followed by a heavy chopping board or a baking tray to press it down. Set aside to press for a few hours, or ideally keep it pressed in the fridge overnight.

Preheat the grill (broiler) on a low setting.

Once your pudding is pressed and cooled, put all the rarebit ingredients into a bowl, season to taste and give them a good whisk. Pour the rarebit mixture over the top of the pudding, then slip it under the preheated grill for about 5–8 minutes until bubbling up and golden – do keep an eye on it! Remove from the grill and serve whilst still hot and gooey – yum!

Pork belly souse

Serves 6–8
Prep time 20 minutes, plus pork pressing time
Cook time 3 hours

My dad used to make souse when I was a kid, and the zing of lemon juice and chilli still rings on my tongue when I think of it. I LOVED it, but went off it when I got older and didn't want to eat all the porky "bits". I am happily over that phase now and love a pig foot! For this version of souse, I use pork belly, which, to me, is the best of both worlds. Pork souse is traditionally eaten with Cornmeal Pudding (see page 154).

For the pork

1.5kg (3lb 3oz) piece of pork belly

4 garlic cloves, peeled

4 whole star anise

1½ tsp crushed juniper berries

10g (⅓oz) coriander (cilantro) stalks

10g (⅓oz) parsley stalks

1½ tsp salt

For the souse

1 tsp black peppercorns

1 tsp coriander seeds

2 Scotch bonnets or bird's-eye chillies, thinly sliced with seeds left in

2 onions, very thinly sliced

2 cucumbers, very thinly sliced

2 spring onions (scallions), green tops only thinly sliced

10g (⅓oz) finely chopped coriander (cilantro) leaves

10g (⅓oz) finely chopped flat leaf parsley

juice of 2 limes

2½ tsp salt

Preheat the oven to 150°C fan (170°C/340°F/Gas 4).

Throw all the pork ingredients into a deep roasting tray and pour over enough water to cover the meat. Cover the tray tightly with tin foil and cook in the preheated oven for 3 hours, or until the meat is tender. Remove from the oven.

Drain the cooking liquid (reserving it for another recipe). Remove the pork belly from the roasting tray and press it by sandwiching the meat between 2 baking trays with something heavy on top. Set aside and allow to cool completely.

Meanwhile, for the souse, crush the black peppercorns and coriander seeds in a pestle and mortar.

Add all the remaining souse ingredients, along with the crushed peppercorns and coriander seeds, to a large bowl and give it a good mix.

Once it is cold, cut the pressed pork into cubes, then drop them into the bowl with all the other souse ingredients. Give it a good stir so the pork is evenly distributed throughout, then leave to sit for at least an hour in the fridge, or overnight if you have the time.

Serve using a slotted spoon. You want all the ingredients, but not the brine, on the plate.

Serve a slice of the cornmeal pudding with the souse tumbled on top. The souse should be lip-stinging fiery. Combine that with the sweetness of the pudding, and it's an explosively delicious brunch dish – try it with a cold beer.

Stout-braised oxtail

Serves 6–8
Prep time 20 minutes, plus marinating time
Cook time 3–3½ hours

I'm always looking for ways to deepen flavour in a pot. When we were in the pub kitchen in Homerton, many beers and ales were experimented with, and this still has to be one of the best applications of ale to food we came up with. The dark richness of the stout and the cartilaginous glory of the oxtail are a match made in heaven.

For the stew

2kg (4½lb) chopped oxtail

generous splash of rapeseed (canola) oil

2 onions, thinly sliced

5 garlic cloves, grated

2 bird's-eye chillies, finely chopped

4 star anise

1 tsp green cardamom pods

3 black cardamom pods

2 litres (8½ cups) beef stock

500ml (generous 2 cups) stout

3 bay leaves

3 cinnamon sticks

1 tbsp blackstrap molasses

3 tbsp dark soy sauce

For the marinade

1 tsp chilli flakes

1 tbsp ground coriander

1 tbsp ground cumin

1 tsp ground turmeric

1 tsp cracked or ground allspice berries

¾ tsp salt

80ml (⅓ cup) rapeseed (canola) oil

Put the chopped oxtail into a big bowl and rinse it under cold running water to remove any small pieces of bone. Drain and pat dry.

Add the chilli flakes, coriander, cumin, turmeric, allspice, salt, and oil to the bowl. Rub the ingredients into the meat with your hands, then leave the oxtail to marinate for at least 3 hours in the fridge, or overnight if you've got time.

Add the splash of rapeseed (canola) oil to a big, deep, heavy-based saucepan and set over a medium heat. Sauté the onions, garlic, and chillies in the oil until translucent. Add the star anise and green and black cardamom and sauté for a further 4–5 minutes.

Add the marinated oxtail and brown the meat until it has a good caramel colour all over. Pour the beef stock and stout into the pan, then add the bay leaves, cinnamon sticks, molasses, and soy sauce. Turn the heat down to medium–low, cover the pan with the lid and gently simmer for around 3–3½ hours, or until the meat is meltingly tender and falling off the bone, and the sauce is glossy and coats the meat.

Serve with rice or Fungee (see page 146).

Sweet things

I must have called my niece Phoebe Oliver about 20 times for this chapter. She is my touchstone when it comes to baking or anything sweet. She is just one of those people with such an instinct for this kind of cooking that the temptation is always to sit back and watch her do it, because it's always beautiful. In the Caribbean we don't really do desserts so much, but boy do we love a sweet treat.

Sunday 7th March

What's for pudding? The cousin with the sweet tooth

Today is my cousin Bernie's birthday. Bernie just loves a dessert. Whenever we go to a restaurant together, she immediately goes to the back of the menu and chooses her sweet course first. She's had an idea to have a tea party for her birthday and I concur that it is indeed an excellent plan.

I will admit that puddings have kind of come to me later in life, due to my innate fear of anything precise or mathematical. Life, however, has a funny way of making one deal with the things we're most scared of, right? And since I've been cooking more "in public" so to speak, I have had to teach myself how to weigh and measure and cook things in a more exacting way. So, the fear of baking or working at that end of the menu gradually subsided, and I have found a whole new world of wonderful.

Today, I've made a brand-new recipe for Bernie. I've gathered limes, coconuts, and condensed milk together and I'm working on a kind of cheesecake tart situation that is looking gooood!

ON THE MENU TODAY

COCONUT & LIME CHEESECAKE

Coconut & lime cheesecake

Serves 12
Prep time 30 minutes, plus setting time

The first sweet things I ever made were cheesecakes – they provide endless opportunities to explore flavour and are easy peasy! This particular iteration brings together the creaminess of white chocolate with toasty coconut and vibrant lime to sublime effect. Not too sweet, jussst right.

For the base

100g (3½oz) gingernut biscuits (ginger snaps)

100g (3½oz) oat biscuits (cookies), such as Hobnobs

50g (⅔ cup) desiccated (dried shredded) coconut, toasted

120g (1 stick) melted unsalted butter

pinch of salt

For the filling

280g (1¼ cups) full-fat cream cheese

4 tbsp coconut condensed milk

200ml (scant 1 cup) coconut milk

150ml (⅔ cup) double (heavy) cream

grated zest and juice of 2 limes

100g (3½oz) white chocolate, melted

For the topping

1 fresh coconut

1 tbsp maple syrup

grated zest of 1 lime

1 fresh mango, peeled, cored, and diced

22–24cm (8–9in) fluted tart tin, base lined with baking parchment

electric hand whisk

Put all the biscuits (ginger snaps and cookies) in a sealable food bag and bash them up to fine crumbs using a rolling pin or similar. Tip the crumbs into a bowl and mix with the toasted coconut, melted butter, and salt. Press into the bottom and sides of the tart tin and chill in the fridge for 1 hour or until set.

Combine all the filling ingredients, apart from the chocolate, in a large mixing bowl. Beat together using an electric hand whisk until smooth and slightly thickened.

Mix through the melted white chocolate. Spoon the filling on top of the set base and chill for a couple of hours in the fridge until set (do note that this cheesecake has quite a soft-set finish).

Meanwhile, preheat the oven to 180°C fan (200°C/400°F/ Gas 6).

Crack open the fresh coconut and peel off flakes of the flesh using a vegetable peeler. You want about 2 handfuls in total. Toss the flakes in the maple syrup and half of the lime zest on a baking tray, then toast in the preheated oven for around 10 minutes until crisp. Leave to cool, then top the cheesecake with the toasted coconut.

Mix together the diced mango and remaining lime zest and serve a little spoon of this alongside slices of cheesecake, or pile it on top of the cheesecake as well.

Bitter chocolate shots with tamarind salt caramel

Serves 8
Prep time 30 minutes, plus cooling/chill time
Cook time 20 minutes

BIG in the game... if you're looking for chocolate you came to the right place. This is another dish from our pub in Homerton days. It's intense and indulgent, with tamarind bringing just the right amount of sour to balance out the sweet. Top with plenty of whipped cream if it takes your fancy (it does mine).

For the caramel

200g (generous ¾ cup) double (heavy) cream

large pinch of salt

300g (1½ cups) caster (superfine) sugar

150g (⅔ cup) salted butter, cold and cubed

2 tbsp tamarind paste

For the mousse

190g (6¾oz) dark (bittersweet) chocolate, chopped

8 eggs, separated, at room temperature

2½ tbsp caster (superfine) sugar

pinch of salt

For the ganache

150g (⅔ cup) double (heavy) cream

pinch of salt

120g (4½oz) dark (bittersweet) chocolate drops with 60% cocoa solids, or grated chocolate

8 decorative serving glasses

electric hand whisk

To make the caramel, warm the cream and salt in a small saucepan over a low heat. Do not let the cream boil.

Meanwhile, place a separate medium saucepan over a low heat and add the sugar. When the sugar starts to melt, stir constantly so that it doesn't burn. If any lumps form, just break them up with your spoon. When all the sugar has melted into an amber liquid, whisk in the warm cream, butter, and tamarind. Cook the caramel gently for 5 minutes, then turn off the heat and let it cool for 30 minutes.

Pour the cooled caramel into the bottom of 8 serving glasses and chill in the fridge while you make the mousse.

For the mousse, gently melt the chocolate in a heatproof bowl set over a pan of just simmering water. Do not let the base of the bowl touch the water. When the chocolate has melted, remove from the heat and leave to cool slightly.

Whisk the egg whites with the sugar to soft peaks using an electric hand whisk. In a separate bowl, mix the salt with half of the egg yolks, saving the rest for another recipe. Beat the egg yolks into the melted chocolate with a spatula.

Fold a third of the whipped egg whites into the chocolate mixture until fully combined. Gently fold the rest of the egg whites into the chocolate, taking care not to knock out too much air. Spoon the chocolate mousse on top of the caramel in the glasses, leaving about 3mm (⅛in) for the ganache layer on top. Chill in the fridge for 4 hours until set.

For the ganache, gently heat the cream and salt in a pan until hot (do not let it boil). Take off the heat and whisk in a third of the chocolate. Pour the cream over the remaining chocolate in a bowl and leave for 2 minutes. Whisk until combined into a smooth ganache. Let cool for 20 minutes.

Top the mousse in the glasses with the ganache and serve.

Tres leches bread & butter pudding

Serves 6
Prep time 10 minutes, plus 15 minutes soaking time
Cook time 35–40 minutes

Oh yes three, count 'em, THREE milks in this bread and butter pudding, inspired by the tres leches cakes that are so popular in Puerto Rico and Mexico. Crisp at the edges, sweet and redolent with vanilla, it really is a treat to behold. If you're having people over, you can make it ahead of time and just flash it in the oven at a high heat before serving. Winning, winning!

For the bread and butter pudding

300–350g (10–12oz) brioche, roughly chopped into cubes (or another enriched bread of your choice – depending on which type you use, you may need to use a little more or less)

80g (⅓ cup) unsalted butter, melted, plus a little extra for greasing

2 whole eggs

2 egg yolks

300ml (1¼ cups) condensed milk

300ml (1¼ cups) evaporated milk

100ml (generous ⅓ cup) full-fat (whole) milk

2 tsp ground cinnamon

2¼ tsp ground nutmeg

whipped vanilla-scented cream or custard, to serve

For the butterscotch sauce

3½ tbsp unsalted butter

200ml (generous ¾ cup) double (heavy) cream

160g (¾ cup) light brown soft sugar

1⅓ tbsp spiced rum

Preheat the oven to 160°C fan (180°C/350°F/Gas 4).

Pile the brioche into a greased baking dish. In a large bowl or jug, stir together all the other pudding ingredients (apart from the cream or custard to serve) so they are very thoroughly mixed.

Pour most of the resulting custard mixture over the brioche, reserving just a little to pour over later. Make sure every bit of the brioche is coated in the custard, then leave to soak for about 15 minutes.

Pour the rest of the custard over the pudding, then slip the dish into the preheated oven and bake for 35–40 minutes, until golden on top.

Meanwhile, make the butterscotch sauce. Melt the butter in a small saucepan over a low heat. Add the cream and sugar, bring the mixture to a simmer, then add the rum. Turn up the heat just a notch or two, and leave the mixture to bubble slightly more vigorously for about 10 minutes. When the sauce is thick enough to coat the back of a spoon, turn off the heat.

Once cooked, leave the pudding to cool a little in the dish. Pour the butterscotch sauce over the top and serve with whipped vanilla-scented cream, or custard.

Rum & raisin bakewell tarts

Serves 10
Prep time 30 minutes, plus soaking and resting time
Cook time 50–55 minutes

This dish really came into being because my father-in-law, Lloyd, keeps asking me for rum and raisin everything, so this is for Lloyd. The gorgeous short pastry is from the mind of she who rules all baking, my niece, Phoebe Oliver. Came out right nice.

For the purée

300g (1¾ cups) raisins

150ml (⅔ cup) dark or golden rum

For the sweet pastry

125g (1 stick plus 1 tbsp) unsalted butter

210g (1½ cups) plain (all-purpose) flour, plus extra for dusting (optional)

75g (⅓ cup plus 2 tsp) caster (superfine) sugar

25g (¼ cup) ground almonds

pinch of salt

2 eggs

For the frangipane

250g (2 sticks) unsalted butter

250g (1¼ cups) caster (superfine) sugar

2 eggs, beaten

250g (2½ cups) ground almonds

a few drops of almond extract

75g (generous ½ cup) plain (all-purpose) flour

3½ tbsp flaked (slivered) almonds

food processor

10 fluted tart tins, about 9cm (3½in)

baking beans (pie weights)

electric hand whisk or stand mixer

To make the purée, soak the raisins in the rum for at least an hour. Blend to a purée in a food processor, then scrape the purée into a bowl and set aside. Wash and dry the food processor for the next step.

For the sweet pastry, add the butter, flour, sugar, ground almonds, and salt to a food processor. Pulse until the mixture looks a bit like breadcrumbs. Tip in the eggs, one by one, pulsing with each addition until the dough has just formed. Form the dough into a ball with your hands, wrap it in cling film (plastic wrap) and chill in the fridge for 2 hours.

Preheat the oven to 170°C fan (190°C/375°F/Gas 5).

Remove the pastry from the fridge, unwrap and place on a lightly floured work surface or between 2 pieces of baking parchment. Use a rolling pin to roll out the dough to the thickness of a 50p coin (roughly 3mm/⅛in).

Using a 12cm (5in) cookie cutter or a bowl of the same size, cut out 10 circles of pastry. Carefully line each of the fluted tart tins with a piece of pastry, making sure it fits snugly into the corners. Pop a piece of baking parchment over each piece of pastry and fill each case with baking beans (pie weights). Blind bake the tart cases in the preheated oven for 25 minutes.

Remove from the oven, remove the beans and paper and let cool slightly. Leave the oven on at the same temperature. Meanwhile, make the frangipane by beating the butter and sugar until pale and fluffy either in a stand mixer with the paddle attachment, or using an electric hand whisk. Beat in the eggs one by one. Add the almond essence, then beat in the ground almonds. Finally, fold in the flour.

Spread a thin layer of the raisin purée into the bottom of each of the tart cases. Divide the frangipane between the tart cases, being careful not to overfill. Top each tart with a few flaked almonds and bake in the preheated oven for 25–30 minutes until golden. Leave the tarts to cool before removing from the cases. Serve with softly whipped cream, if you like.

Black cake

Serves 12
Prep time 20 minutes, plus soaking time
Cook time 1 hour 50 minutes

Also known as Caribbean Christmas cake, you will find this pretty much everywhere across the region as the centrepiece at the end of most celebration tables. With dark fruit steeped in rum and spices, it is soft, moist and decidedly moreish. The longer you can leave your fruit to soak at the start, the juicier it will be.

225g (8oz) prunes

550g (1¼lb) raisins

500ml (generous 2 cups) dark rum, for soaking

225g (2 sticks) butter

150g (1¼ cups) caster (granulated) sugar

4 large (US grade A large) eggs

4 tbsp Caribbean browning sauce

1 tsp vanilla extract, or seeds from 1 vanilla pod

½ tsp ground allspice

1 tsp ground cinnamon

½ tsp salt

1 tsp baking powder

200g (1½ cups) plain (all-purpose) flour

electric hand whisk or stand mixer

food processor

23cm (9in) cake tin, greased and lined with baking parchment

Start by soaking the prunes and raisins in the dark rum for a minimum of 2 days. The longer you soak it the better.

Preheat the oven to 160°C fan (180°C/350°F/Gas 4).

Using an electric hand whisk or stand mixer, cream together the butter and sugar until light and fluffy. In a separate bowl, beat the eggs with the browning sauce and vanilla. Slowly pour the egg mixture into the creamed butter and sugar, mixing until combined.

Drain the soaked fruit, then take half of the soaked fruit and blitz it up in a food processor. Roughly chop the remaining soaked fruit, then add this to the batter along with the blended soaked fruit, the spices, and salt. Give it all a good stir to combine. Gradually fold in the flour and baking powder.

Pour the mixture into the prepared cake tin, cover with tin foil and slip into the preheated oven for about 1 hour 50 minutes. Check the cake from time to time, as baking times may vary. Stick a clean knife into the middle of the cake – it's ready when the knife comes out clean, or almost clean.

Leave to cool slightly, then remove from the cake tin. Serve at celebrations all year round.

Uncle Arnold's pear, rum, & sultana cake

My uncle Arnold passed away recently, a man I loved dearly. He taught me how to drink good rum and he was a gardener most magnificent. So, to honour him and his wife, my wonderful and most beloved Aunt Enid, I have devised a pudding that incorporates the last pears I picked from his garden and, of course, plenty of honeyed golden rum.

Serves 6–8
Prep time 40 minutes, plus overnight soaking
Cook time 2½ hours

250g (1½ cups) sultanas (golden raisins)

350ml (1½ cups) golden rum

1 tsp mixed spice (pumpkin pie spice)

1⅓ tbsp vanilla extract

4 Conference (or Bosc) pears

450g (2 cups) unsalted butter, softened

250g (1¼ cups) demerara (Turbinado) sugar

100g (3½oz) stem ginger from a jar of preserved ginger in syrup

400g (14oz) dates, pitted

230g (scant 1¼ cups) caster (granulated) sugar

2 eggs

400g (3 cups) self-raising flour

2 tsp baking powder

80g (3oz) gingernut biscuits (ginger snaps)

whipped cream or custard, to serve

tall 23cm (9in) cake tin, lined with baking parchment

food processor (optional)

electric hand whisk (optional)

Put the sultanas in a large bowl and cover with 250ml (1 cup plus 1 tablespoon) of the golden rum. Stir in the mixed spice and half of the vanilla extract. Leave to soak at room temperature for a minimum of 3 hours or overnight.

Peel the pears and slice them into quarters lengthways. Remove the cores and any seeds. Arrange the pears in the bottom of the lined cake tin in a fan shape or whichever way you fancy. Set aside.

Melt 200g (generous ¾ cup) of the butter with the brown sugar and the remaining 100ml (⅓ cup plus 1 tablespoon) rum in a saucepan over a gentle heat, stirring occasionally. When the sugar has melted and combined with the butter, pour two-thirds of the syrup over the pears to cover them.

Preheat the oven to 150°C fan (170°C/340°F/Gas 4).

Drain the rum-soaked sultanas, saving the rum to use in another recipe. Spoon the stem ginger with a little syrup from the jar into a food processor and add the dates. Blitz briefly (alternatively, you can roughly chop these ingredients by hand). Mix the raisins and chopped or blitzed ginger and dates together in a bowl.

In a separate bowl, beat the remaining butter and caster sugar using an electric hand whisk or a wooden spoon until pale and fluffy. Beat in the eggs, one by one, until evenly combined. Tip in the chopped fruit and beat again. Finally, beat in the flour and baking powder until thoroughly mixed.

Pile the cake mixture into the cake tin on top of the pears and syrup and give the tin a gentle shake from side to side to even out the mixture, or use a spatula or the back of a spoon to smooth it down and allow to settle.

Crush the ginger biscuits (ginger snaps) to a crumb with a rolling pin or in a food processor and sprinkle over the top of the settled cake mixture. Cover the cake tin with a sheet of tin foil and slip into the preheated oven for about 2 hours 30 minutes, or until a skewer inserted comes out clean.

Remove the cake from the oven and leave to cool in the tin. Once cooled, run a knife around the edge of the cake. Lay a large plate on top of the tin, then tip it upside down and the whole thing should come out. Gently peel back the paper, pour over the remaining syrup and serve slices of the cake with whipped cream or custard.

Rice pudding

Serves 4
Prep time 10–20 minutes
Cook time 20-30 minutes

Rice pudding in all its forms, hot, cold, or baked, is hugely popular in the Caribbean and I'm a big fan. My dear friend Matthew Fort once told me that his mother always added pillows of whipped cream just before serving, and I can confirm it's a particularly great idea! I like to top this rice pudding with some rum-soaked prunes and raisins to ring the changes, and yes, I think it's also an excellent plan.

250g (1⅓ cups) short-grain pudding rice or jasmine rice

½ tsp salt, or more to taste

2 cinnamon sticks

1–2 tsp grated fresh ginger or ginger powder, to taste

2 cardamom pods

1 tsp whole or ground allspice

250ml (1 cup plus 1 tbsp) full-fat dairy or non-dairy milk, plus a splash extra as needed

½ x 400ml (13.5fl oz) can of sweetened coconut milk or condensed milk

1 tsp vanilla extract

sweetener of your choice, to taste (such as coconut sugar, cinnamon, light brown sugar, honey, or agave syrup, etc.)

Optional additions

2 tbsp unsalted butter

100g (⅔ cup) raisins (soaked in rum, if you like)

For the topping (optional)

maple syrup

toasted nuts

toasted coconut flakes

rum-soaked prunes and raisins (see page 260)

Place the rice into a medium–large saucepan along with 550ml (2⅓ cups) of water, the salt, cinnamon sticks, ginger, cardamom pods, allspice, and butter (if using). Set over a medium heat and cook for about 10–15 minutes, stirring occasionally, until the rice is just tender with a little bite to it.

Add the dairy or non-dairy milk, reduce the heat to low and cook the mixture for another 10 minutes, stirring from time to time, until the milk has been mostly absorbed. Add the sweetened coconut milk or condensed milk, adjusting the moisture with extra dairy milk, if needed, until perfectly creamy.

Remove from the heat, then carefully take out the whole spices and stir in the vanilla, raisins (if using) and sweetener of your choice. Set aside to cool slightly before serving with toppings of your choice. Try maple syrup, toasted nuts or coconut flakes, and/or the rum-soaked prunes and raisins used in the Black Cake recipe (see page 260).

Wednesday 10th March

A visit with Maya Angelou – a closing essay

I have just started reading a book called *The Cooking Gene* by Michael W. Twitty. My God it's extraordinary, I feel like I'm meeting an old friend and picking up a conversation that I've been having with myself and anyone else that will listen for a good few years now. I am reminded of the day I met one of my all-time goddess heroines, the stunningly brilliant Maya Angelou.

My dear friend Nick Reding and I went to her house to interview her for a project we were working on. She was everything you would want her to be; regal, gracious, witty, fascinating, elegant, poetic, and enchanting. After the interview, she invited us back to her house for dinner. Needless to say we were thrilled and, of course, dutifully turned up on time at her door. The evening was like a dream – we sat with her in her gazebo in the garden whilst she told us stories of Quincy Jones and cicadas in that voice, that VOICE... I was transfixed by her. Then we went in for dinner.

At this point I should say that Ms Angelou and all of us had a good "few" glasses of wine under our belts, and the conversation quite energetically turned to one of identity. She asked me about my family and where we came from. I, of course, spoke of Antigua and then said, "but I am also English". There was a pause, and she looked me dead in the eye and said "Well that's just stupid! Why would you claim to be from a place that doesn't want you? You're not exactly what they mean when they describe an English rose." At the time, it was like a punch to the stomach, and I did feel a bit stupid. I tried weakly to argue my point, that in fact I think I am EXACTLY what an English rose can look like! We are brown, black, blonde, and everything in between. I'm pretty sure she wasn't convinced, and I have to say she got a bit moody (good old white wine grumpy really). We left a tad deflated after having had the MOST magical of days. We shook it off and concentrated on the good stuff and sort of drew a veil over the weird moment, but in the back of my head it always bothered me. It took me a while, but I think I now understand what happened (apart from a LOT of wine!).

NOW, I tell this story because I realized later that being a FIRST generation immigrant is a very difficult position to understand if you don't occupy it (no matter how massive your brain and talent is). There is such specificity. You're not exactly from where your parents have travelled from, although you carry it in your skin and your soul and on your face and indeed on your palate. It is in the flavours and textures you crave. However, you're not fully from the place they travelled TO either. You're something new, something not necessarily understood yet by you or anyone else. I realize that even she, Maya Angelou the goddess genius didn't quite get it. I think in so many ways, I am only starting to really understand it myself.

This trip has been central to that understanding. I'm here for long enough to feel at home, to truly feel the Antiguan in me and understand it. And yet whilst I am in some way revenant, I am also a visitor. An English visitor, one who has brought back something in my spirit that my parents left with. Perhaps that is hope, light, and the promise of the new. That's what I was trying to explain to the glorious Ms Angelou, and what I've been trying to understand myself for quite some years.

This, I think, informs my cooking. The old traditions are here in Antigua, and they are spectacular. I am entranced when I meet someone like Sister Hector or cook with my brilliant cousin Juni, who has spent so many of his formative years here and is privy to the old school ways. But for me, I have to sing my new song too. I am striving to honour those old ways and traditions and bring them to join hands with new ideas as well.

Tonight, I'm going old school. I'm going to make one of my mum's favourite dishes, which in itself has a fascinating, complex, but simply explained origin; to create the new, you must know the old.

ON THE MENU TODAY

VINIDALOUSH

Vinidaloush

Serves 6–8
Prep time 20 minutes, plus overnight marination and resting time
Cook time 3 hours

2.4kg (5¼lb) pork belly, deboned, skin on, skin and flesh scored

2 large pinches of sea salt

freshly ground black pepper

For the marinade

200ml (scant 1 cup) sherry vinegar

350ml (1½ cups) golden rum

5 tbsp Green Seasoning (see page 110)

2 tsp ground allspice

4 bird's-eye chillies, thinly sliced

1 tsp cumin seeds

1 tsp coriander seeds

For the sauce

pork cooking juices

remaining marinade

150ml (⅔ cup) golden rum

2 tbsp clear honey

120g (1 stick) cold unsalted butter

My mother was the one who introduced me to this recipe. She kept telling me she really wanted vinidaloush and I had never heard of it, so I delved into the collective family memory bank, which essentially means calling my cousin Baden Prince (known to us as Juni), who is a brilliant Antiguan cook and poet, and remembers every recipe anyone has ever shown him! It's truly a dish that encapsulates so much of what is innate within the Caribbean kitchen.

The influences of the dish go back to Portugal, to vinha d'alhos, which marinates meat in vinegar and garlic, which then connects to Goa in India and vindaloo, a dish that I can't imagine anyone is not familiar with, which also marinates meat in vinegar and spices. Then in Antigua and other islands in the Caribbean, we have vinidaloush, sometimes also called garlic pork, in which we use sherry vinegar and garlic to marinate the meat before cooking. This dish to me fully and completely joins up so many of those footsteps I spoke about at the beginning of the book. The feet that have made their way across the region, sometimes as friend, more oftentimes as foe, and whatever the guise, always leaving their mark in our food and on our plates.

Place the pork belly in a large bowl and combine the marinade ingredients in a separate bowl. Pour the marinade over the pork, making sure it is coated all over. Cover the bowl with cling film (plastic wrap) and leave the pork in the fridge to marinate overnight.

The next day, preheat the oven to 120°C fan (140°C/285°F/ Gas 1).

Remove the pork belly from the marinade and transfer it to a board, reserving the bowl of marinade. Rub the salt into the scored skin of the pork belly. Set a heavy-based, wide frying pan over a high heat until it is almost smoking-hot. Lay the pork belly into the pan folded in half, skin-side down and sear until you get a good colour all over, turning the belly so that both sides get evenly seared.

Transfer the pork belly to a roasting tray, skin-side down. Spoon a couple of tablespoons of the reserved marinade over the scored flesh and give it a couple of grinds of black pepper. Slip the roasting tray into the preheated oven and roast for 3 hours, checking in on the pork every hour and spooning over a little more of the marinade. When the meat is completely tender, remove from the oven, transfer the pork belly to a board, cover with tin foil and leave to rest for at least 30 minutes.

When you are nearly ready to serve, take the pork cooking juices from the pan and what is left of the marinade and pour both into a large, wide frying pan. Set over a medium heat and let the mixture bubble up. Add the rum, honey, and a splash of water and bubble for a few more minutes. Finally, add the butter and bubble for another few minutes, then remove the sauce from the heat.

Carve the meat when it has rested, then pour the sauce from the pan back over the succulent meat to serve.

Index

My girls

Gosh, it's been a while since I felt like I had some slow time in the kitchen. Time to pull at the strands of ideas and have a little potter around. I'm now up in Stratford-upon-Avon for the next three months filming, so at weekends I have space and time and air to breathe. My dear girls came last night. My daughter, Miquita, and my niece, my brother's daughter Phoebe. It's so lovely to have them here with me, just the sound of their voices and laughing and cosiness floating through the house makes me feel so rooted and at home wherever we are. The sound of those girls has been around me for nearly 38 years, and without them life feels oddly off-key.

Miquita has been filming, too, and running up and down in that there London working like a Trojan, a nd she needs to just stop for a minute. Phoebe, who is the most inspired baker I know, works and lives near Toulouse in France, so we haven't seen her for nearly 2 years – what with all the world being upside down for so long! She is finally here and it's making me AND Miquita AND her so happy, we need each other like a body needs water! We are about to start working together on illustrations (Phoebe is also an amazing artist) and sweet things for this book. Today I am going to make us all a lunch.

Last night I brined small chickens in Earl Grey tea and accented the bergamot with some other citrus, a spot of lemon verbena, garlic, soft fresh thyme, rosemary, and some other bits. I've also just made a spice rub, and the chickens are sitting waiting to go into the oven for a long, slow cook. I've got some winter roots to fritter, a broth to make and a baked pumpkin cornmeal porridge to be infused with coconut and finished with a butter. I'm going to salt and drench some little baby cucumbers in lemon like my mum always used to do... we'll see what else comes out of the day. I feel that lovely, leisurely Saturday in the kitchen peace. I can do what I like, get some tunes on and float off into my soul healing time.

And then comes Sunday. I have all the leftovers from yesterday and a long working week stretching ahead. I feel ready to make a 4-day soup – this will require the big pot! I will start with the chicken leftovers from yesterday, throwing them in with an onion, some leftover carrot bits, herb stalks and leaves all from yesterday's cooking. Cover all of it with water, add a bulb of garlic and a whole chilli. Now the soup will simmer gently, drawing all the flavours from the end of that succulent chicken and all the accompanying bits and bobs. This soup is the perfect opportunity to have a little fridge harvest... is there anything else in there you thought you were going to use this week and it didn't quite happen? Chuck it in the soup pot. This is my way of avoiding waste and getting maximum flavour into my every which way soup/ stock for the week ahead.

25/12/88

Sean

There are times in life when we're just in pain. Our souls are crying out for succour, we've lost someone we love, and it feels like life will never move in quite the same way again. We are right, of course, it won't. That's not to say that life won't go on, it will, but it will be different; irrevocably changed.

When my beautiful brother Sean died, my world cracked. My heart nearly stopped beating with the shock of it and my soul froze. I've been thinking about him a lot these last few days, thinking about family and what it means to me. Even as I write these words, the pain comes back to me viscerally. When it happened all those years ago, someone said to me, "You won't ever get over it, but you'll find some place to keep it." This was the only thing that made any sense to me, and it has proved to be true. There is a small place inside of me that holds him close, and every now and again something will trigger that sadness and it all comes rushing up. I am so grateful that we had him for the time that we did, he was the most amazing of men!

A brilliant and inspired bass player and producer, a devastatingly handsome philandering terrible boyfriend, a loving dad and uncle. He adored his children, our darling ones Phoebe and Theo, and my daughter Miquita. He was an excellent mate and a hilarious, charming, compelling cheeky human. He lived more in his 27 years than some people do in 90, and that is the way the world turns I guess. When he died, we cooked and we cooked and we cooked, it seemed like the only thing to do. Food was and is the language of loss and simultaneously comfort. Sean loved a dark, meaty stew of ANY kind, and he LOVED a sweet potato! So that is what goes in the pot whenever I think of him.

Thank you

Writing this book has been a dream come true. Books of all kinds have sustained me throughout my whole life. I am thankful to so many people who have helped me turn a dream into a reality.

The first is my mother, the wonder that is Maria Oliver. She took me to the library regularly when I was a child, and it has enriched my world. My mother, a brilliant educator to so many, taught me that words matter, that writing and reading have the power to transform a life. She showed me how to cook and live in a way that connects me to family, and that family is whatever you decide it is. She taught me to seek my own heart's voice and love in everything that I do. A truly remarkable woman who dances (yes dances not marches) to the beat of her own drum and who has always taught me to do the same. Thank you, mum, for showing me how to be brave, how to dance and how to always be true to myself.

I want to thank my amazing daughter Miquita Oliver for being my team and my anchor, from the moment you were born. I don't know when you got so wise, but I'm so grateful for it and so proud of you. Thank you for always seeing me, for helping me to be kind to myself and making me realize when I need to rest and when I need to push forward – even when I don't know how I'm going to get there.

Thank you to my dearest love, Garfield. The kindest man I know and my partner in life and all things. Without your constant love, patience, ideas, and support I don't know where I'd be, and of course thanks for being my self-appointed food muse/idiot!

Thank you to the glorious Kelly Miles, my sister, my friend, and my right-hand woman. Without Kelly, nothing would ever happen. Thank you for being by my side every step of the way. I would not have been able to make sense of this writing without you and your logical, organized mind. And of course thank you for being SO hilarious!

A huge double thank you is due to my exceptionally talented niece, Phoebe Oliver. Firstly for working on all of the sweet things in this book with me – your skill as a pastry chef is such a beauty to behold. I learn so much from you in that part of the kitchen every time we work. Secondly, thank you for your gentle, meditative, stunning illustrations. It's quite astonishing that you can do BOTH of these things so well, I'm so proud of you and your dad would be too.

Thank you to Jessica Stone, my genius agent and sister. You truly are a tiny magnificent wonder in my life. Thank you for your clear, calm vision, fire and brimstone. I'm so grateful for you all... Grace O'Leary, Flora Webber, and everyone at ITG.

Thank you to my fabulous cousin and brilliantly talented chef Sulaiman Leblanc-Prince for all your work on the Wadadli team, and for the thorough and detailed research on the heritage recipes so that we could get them right where we needed them to be.

Thank you to all the Wadadli Kitchen team, past and present, for working with me so closely on our Wadadli recipes. Particularly to Sacha Henry, who I'm still playing culinary table tennis with and who is still with me. Also a special thank you to Randel Benain in the past for your inspiration, creativity, and talent.

Thank you to everyone at Dorling Kindersley for shepherding me through this entire process. It's all so new to me. I'm so grateful to Max Pedliham, Katie Cowan, Cara Armstrong, Kiron Gill, Alice Sambrook and all of you for your patience, support, and enthusiasm for my work. Thank you must also go to the brilliant Stephanie Milner who reeled me in to DK with her boundless energy and love for the project in the beginning.

Thank you to the excellent, patient, and talented chef Alex Gray for working with me so closely on testing all these recipes and helping me to feel confident in my creativity and my clarity.

I must also thank the wonderful Robert Billington for his beautiful photography, his mastery of light and shadow, his energy, and not forgetting his brilliant appetite! Thank you also to the marvellous Nicole Gomes for your skill, musical appreciation, and attention to detail, and of course to lovely Jack Storer for your thoughtful and careful work. Thanks must also go to the inspired Rachel Vere who knows how to shift a spoon an inch and change an entire energy, she seemed to magically understand my doily obsession and all the little tchotchkes and things I love and bring them to the table. You guys were a joy to work with, seeing my food in such an array of beautiful settings was hugely emotional for me and I'm truly grateful to you.

Thanks to the brilliant Dave Brown for your talent, painstaking attention to detail, and for listening and absorbing my quite random references and bringing them into such a beautiful coherent design.

Thanks are due to the wonderful and supremely talented make-up artist Kellie Jo Licorish and brilliantly inspired stylist Shara Johnson, who are with me through thick and thin and hold me up when I'm dropping with exhaustion, making me look fabulous even when I'm feeling exactly the opposite.

Thank you always and forever to my three guardian angels, who came into my life at a time when I was really very broken, when my heart had nearly stopped beating, and who held me close and brought me back to life with love, patience, laughter, and tenderness. Nick Reding, Sandra Kane, and Eammon Walker – I love you all forever. Without all of you there would be no me.

Lastly, I want to thank all my friends and family who have steadfastly encouraged me over the years to keep cooking and to keep reaching for both the moon AND the stars.

About the author

Award-winning TV chef and broadcaster Andi Oliver enjoys a rich and varied career, with food and music being at the forefront throughout.

Andi first rose to fame fronting the band Rip Rig + Panic with Neneh Cherry in 1981, before going on to establish a career in TV. She has fronted many shows on music, popular culture, and food, including *The Truth About Food* and *Neneh and Andi Dish It Up* for the BBC.

Most recently, Andi has been a judge on the BBC's *Great British Menu* for four series. She presented the festive special in December 2020 and since then, much to the delight of viewers, has become the regular host and presenter of the popular series, supporting the chefs through the heat of the kitchen.

On air, you can find Andi as a frequent panel member on BBC Radio 4's *The Kitchen Cabinet* alongside Jay Rayner, as well as a contributor to Radio 4's award-winning *The Food Programme*. She also followed in the footsteps of Yotam Ottolenghi as Head Judge alongside Sheila Dillon for the BBC's prestigious *Food & Farming Awards*.

Outside the realm of food, Andi hosted *Jazz 365* for BBC4, with the production winning Best Music Programme at the Broadcast Awards. After hosting the Cheltenham Literature Festival for Sky Arts, Andi will soon be hosting the third live book series for Sky Arts, alongside best-selling novelist Elizabeth Day.

Along with her daughter Miquita Oliver, Andi took part in travel programme *Eight Go Rallying: The Road to Saigon* in 2018 for BBC2. 2021 saw the duo hit the road again to film *The Caribbean with Andi and Miquita* for the BBC, this time embarking on a life-changing journey of personal and social exploration across Antigua, Barbuda, and subsequently Barbados. The two films have been a massive hit, attracting huge audiences across a transgenerational and transcultural demographic.

Throughout her colourful career, Andi has always come back to her work in the kitchen, perfecting her skill as a chef and getting involved with exciting food-related ventures. She ran a successful ephemeral restaurant – The Moveable Feast – for four years and was then creative director of The Birdcage Pub on Columbia Road before launching her own kitchen at The Jackdaw and Star pub in Homerton. She opened her award-winning restaurant – Andi's – in 2016 and 2020 saw her create her newest food project, Wadadli Kitchen. Here, Andi seeks to shine a light on real Caribbean home-cooking and create powerful conversations about exploring identity and migration through cultural exchange projects.

DK US
Publishing Director Katie Cowan
Art Director Maxine Pedliham
Editorial Director Cara Armstrong
Senior Acquisitions Editor Stephanie Milner
Senior Designer Louise Brigenshaw
Project Editor Kiron Gill
Jackets Coordinator Jasmin Lennie
Senior Production Editor Tony Phipps
Senior Production Controller Stephanie McConnell

Editor Alice Sambrook
Designer Dave APE
Proofreader John Friend
Indexer Ruth Ellis
Recipe Developer and Food Stylist Alex Gray
Prop Stylist Rachel Vere
Recipe photography Robert Billington
Location photography Tom Mattey
Illustrations Phoebe Oliver

First American Edition, 2023
Published in the United States by DK Publishing
1745 Broadway, 20th Floor, New York, NY 10019

Copyright © 2023 Dorling Kindersley Limited
DK, a Division of Penguin Random House LLC
23 24 25 26 27 10 9 8 7 6 5 4 3 2 1
001–328864–May/2023

All rights reserved.
No part of this publication may be reproduced, stored
in or introduced into a retrieval system, or transmitted,
in any form, or by any means (electronic, mechanical,
photocopying, recording, or otherwise), without the prior
written permission of the copyright owner.
Published in Great Britain by Dorling Kindersley Limited

A catalog record for this book
is available from the Library of Congress.
ISBN: 978-0-7440-7078-1

Printed and bound in China

For the curious
www.dk.com

YA YA

"YA YA seeks out original voices to elevate
and empower, bringing them into the
mainstream where they belong.
The Pepperpot Diaries is the first book to
be published in collaboration with YA YA."

Food note for US readers
Unlike self-raising flour in the UK, self-rising flour
in the US usually has added salt. You can make
your own to keep salt levels down by adding
1 teaspoon of baking powder per each 150g
(1 cup) of plain (all-purpose) flour.

This book was made with Forest
Stewardship Council™ certified
paper – one small step in DK's
commitment to a sustainable future.
**For more information go to
www.dk.com/our-green-pledge**